# china
## land of dragons and emperors

# ALSO BY ADELINE YEN MAH

FOR YOUNG ADULTS
*Chinese Cinderella*
*Chinese Cinderella and the Secret Dragon Society*

FOR ADULTS
*Falling Leaves*
*Watching the Tree*
*A Thousand Pieces of Gold*

# china
*land of dragons and emperors*

## ADELINE YEN MAH

delacorte press

*Sincere thanks to my Australian publisher, Erica Wagner,
who commissioned this book; and to my editor, Sarah Brenan,
who lived through the writing process with me.*

Published in the United States by Delacorte Press, an imprint of Random House
Children's Books, a division of Random House, Inc., New York. Originally published in
paperback in Australia by Allen & Unwin, Sydney, 2008.

Delacorte Press is a registered trademark and the colophon is a trademark of
Random House, Inc.

Visit us on the Web! www.randomhouse.com/teens
Educators and librarians, for a variety of teaching tools, visit us at
www.randomhouse.com/teachers

*Library of Congress Cataloging-in-Publication Data*
Mah, Adeline Yen.
China : land of dragons and emperors / by Adeline Yen Mah.
p. cm.
Includes bibliographical references and index.
ISBN 978-0-385-73748-7 (trade hc : alk. paper)–ISBN 978-0-385-90669-2 (glb : alk. paper)–
ISBN 978-0-375-89099-4 (e-book)  I. China–History–Juvenile literature. I. Title.
II. Title: Land of dragons and emperors.
DS735.M307 2009
951–dc22
2008035331

Printed in the United States of America
10 9 8 7 6 5 4 3 2 1
First American Edition

This book is dedicated to my husband, Bob,
for his support and for making
everything worthwhile.

# CONTENTS

# TO THE READER

I bring you gifts from China: treasures more enchanting than pearls, more precious than jade. Among these pages you will find tales of dragons and emperors, battles and love affairs.

Did you know paper was first made in China? So were the wheelbarrow, crossbow, matches, silk, seismograph, gunpowder, cast iron, stirrups for horses, porcelain, printing and many other wonderful inventions. China's history is also full of larger-than-life people: warlords, emperors, concubines, eunuchs, fierce women.

I'll tell you about the six families who ruled China during the last two millennia, where they came from and their family secrets. We'll explore underground tombs, sacred caves full of ancient statues, royal palaces, the Silk Road and the Great Wall.

This short book holds my personal list of the most fascinating people from China. Their stories have enthralled me throughout my life. If knowledge gained from history is the truest education, then this book is the best present I can give you.

So how can we find out about Chinese history? As it happens, Chinese history is better documented than the history of any other country. From the time of the Han Dynasty 2200 years ago, each court historian kept a diary of current events. These diaries were compiled into a national history, which was kept secret.

A dynasty is a period of time when members of the same family ruled China. The emperor of each new dynasty would appoint his own historians to write an account of the preceding dynasty. This *Standard History* was made available to the public. Today there are 3600 volumes of China's *Standard History*. The last of the series was published in 1986 in Taiwan.

During the last 2200 years, there have been only six major dynasties. Those dynasties, and the Communist rulers of the twentieth century, are the subject of this book. It is well known that Chinese history goes back

much further, to at least 5000 years ago. The early period is summarised in a chart on pages 231–4.

Francis Bacon, the English philosopher known as the 'Father of the Scientific Revolution', wrote in 1620 that there were 'three world-changing inventions: printing, gunpowder and the compass. The first transformed literature, the second warfare, and the third navigation.' He died without knowing that all three had come from China.

Presently, one-fifth of the world's population is Chinese, totalling over 1300 million people. There are more Chinese learning English today than all the native English speakers on Earth. One day China could become the number one English-speaking nation as well as the world's largest manufacturer and consumer. Perhaps it is time to know something about China.

# ENTER THE DRAGON

Let's start before recorded history in
the mythical times when dragons were
supposed to exist. They were said to
have the eyes of a demon and the claws
of an eagle. They were associated
with power over water, with the lucky
number nine and with royalty.

# POWER OVER STORMS

The Chinese dragon is a mythical animal which is connected with water and rainfall. In times of drought, government ministers used to offer sacrifices to the dragon and pray for rain. Dragons are also supposed to have power over moving bodies of water such as rip-tides, storms and tornadoes. They fly by magic and occasionally show themselves as twisters or waterspouts.

Chinese legend says a fish saw a beautiful mountain one day and decided to swim to the top. It fought its way upstream, struggled against rapids, overcame waterfalls and finally reached the summit. There it found the stream blocked by a locked gate. Undaunted, the fish jumped over the gate and was immediately transformed into a dragon. Thus an ordinary fish can turn into a dragon if it tries hard enough. (Many waterfalls in China are named Dragon's Gate.)

We now think that the dragon idea may have been inspired by the giant Yangzi Alligator, or *tu long* (earth dragon) which lives in the lower Yangzi River and can grow to a length of nearly 2 metres (6 feet). The alligator is sensitive to changes in air pressure and appears to know when rain is coming.

## EMPEROR'S SYMBOL

Chinese children were told that when the Yellow Emperor died, he became a dragon and flew into Heaven. From then on, the yellow dragon with five claws on each foot became a symbol of imperial power. The Emperor's throne was called the Dragon Throne and his robe the Dragon Robe. Only the Emperor was allowed to wear clothes embroidered with a yellow dragon. In ancient times, any person who dared to wear such robes without permission was suspected of treason and might even be executed.

## NINE IN ONE

The number 9, the largest single digit, is associated with the dragon (as well as the Emperor) in Chinese minds. It is a lucky number in China because it is pronounced the same as another word, *jiu*, which means a long time or long life. The dragon is supposed to have 117 scales – 81 Yang (or male) scales and 27 Yin (or female) scales. All these numbers are multiples of nine.

Scholar Wang Fu during the Han Dynasty wrote that the dragon had the characteristics of nine different animals. It had the horns of a deer, the head of a camel, the eyes of a demon, the neck of a snake, the belly of a clam, the scales of a carp, the claws of an eagle, the soles of a tiger and the ears of a cow.

The dragon was said to have nine children. Each had a different temperament. A musical dragon would adorn a two-stringed Chinese violin (*erhu*); one which quarrelsome would appear on the handle of a sword; one which was scholarly would be carved on a tombstone; one which liked to jump was placed on the corner of a roof; one which liked to eat would be on chopsticks; one which rode would be on a saddle; one which painted would be on a brush; one which liked water would be on the stern of a boat; and one which liked to run would decorate shoes.

There are many places in China named Nine Dragons. The most famous is probably Kowloon (Nine Dragon) Peninsula, across the harbour from Hong Kong Island. The Nine Dragon Wall is a famous wall in the garden of the Forbidden Palace in Beijing.

## ZODIAC

The Dragon is one of the twelve animals of the Chinese zodiac. People born in 1952, 1964, 1976, 1988 and 2000 were all born in the Year of the Dragon. Dragon people are energetic, popular, fun-loving, honest and brave. They appear stubborn, but are soft-hearted and sensitive. They are most compatible with people born in the Year of the Rat, the Snake, the Monkey or the Rooster.

## PROTEST

For thousands of years, the dragon has been a symbol of the Chinese people. Some Chinese call themselves 'sons of the dragon'. The dragon is part of the logo of Hong Kong.

Although few Chinese now believe that the dragon is a divine creature, it is still tactful not to disfigure or degrade a dragon in China. Recently, an advertisement showed the famous American NBA basketball player Lebron James killing a dragon and defeating two *feitian* (flying women). It was censored by the Chinese government after massive public protest, including an objection from Yao Ming, a Chinese superstar who plays for the Houston Rockets.

# THE POWER OF NUMBERS: WHY 14-YEAR-OLDS ARE UNLUCKY!

We've seen that dragons are associated with the lucky number nine. Are there other lucky numbers? The answer is yes.

Do you know why the Summer Olympics in Beijing were scheduled to open on 8 August 2008 at 8.08.08 p.m. (or 8 minutes and 8 seconds past 8 o'clock)? That's because the number 8 is another lucky number in Chinese culture. The word for 'eight' in the Cantonese dialect sounds like a word meaning 'to prosper' or 'sudden fortune' and is super-lucky to the Chinese.

Many Chinese people pay huge sums of money to buy lucky numbers for their licence plate, telephone number and home address. In Chengdu the telephone number 8888-8888 sold for more than US$250 000. Someone in Hangzhou offered to sell his licence plate A88888 for over one million *yuan*.

The number 6 is also considered lucky in China. The word for 6 *(liu)* sounds like a word that means 'flowing freely' or 'everything will go smoothly'. Because of this, the number 666 is considered one of the luckiest numbers in Chinese culture. It is often displayed in shop windows and neon signs. Licence plate AW6666 was recently sold for 272 000 *yuan* (US$34 000) in an auction to an anonymous bidder in Guangzhou.

The number 4 is considered *un*lucky because four in

Chinese is the word *sì* and sounds like the Chinese word for death. Some hotels in China do not have a fourth floor. A few skyscrapers in Hong Kong have no floors with the number 4 (4, 14, 24, 34, 40–49, 54, 64, 74, 84 and 94) in them. So a tall building with a 100th-floor penthouse might only have 81 floors.

The unluckiest number of all is the number 14, because it sounds like *yao si* (want to die) in Mandarin and *sut se* (bound to die) in Cantonese.

Some hotels in western cities such as New York and London have no 13th floor because 13 is an unlucky number in the West. I once stayed on the 20th floor of a hotel in Hong Kong that combined East and West – the 4th, 13th and 14th floors were all missing. The so-called 20th floor was actually the 17th floor.

*Chinese lucky silk knot with coin charms*

# WASTED WHITE AND LUCKY RED: WHAT COLOURS MEAN IN CHINA

In ancient China, there were five primary colours: red, black, green, white and yellow. These colours corresponded to the five elements (fire, water, wood, metal, earth) and five directions. On old Chinese maps, south was shown at the top and north at the bottom. The fifth 'direction' was the centre, where the country of China was placed. China (*Zhong Guo*) means Middle Kingdom.

**Red** (*hong*) is the colour of fire. It corresponds to summer and the South. It also symbolises success, happiness and good luck.

❋ When a baby is one month old, he is given his name during a Red Egg Ceremony. Eggs are dyed red and given to friends and relatives at a banquet. The baby's forehead is rubbed with a red egg and a bit of his hair is cut off and saved by his mother.
❋ During Chinese New Year, children are given lucky red envelopes (*hong bao*) containing money.
❋ Red is the colour of celebration at birthdays and weddings. In old China, the bride always wore a red dress and rode in a red sedan chair.
❋ Stock-market gains and dividends are often sent in red envelopes.
❋ Gifts are wrapped in red paper to bring good luck.

**Black** (*hei*) is the colour of water. It corresponds to winter and the North. It symbolises Heaven in *The Book of Changes* (*Yi Jing*), believed to be the oldest book in the world. Black was the favourite colour of the First Emperor of China. He made black his official colour. Uniforms, flags and banners at his court were all in black.

**Green** (*lu*) is the colour of plants, trees and woods. It corresponds to spring and the East and has a strange meaning in China. A man who 'wears a green hat' has a wife who is cheating on him. Chinese men avoid green hats – especially if they have beautiful wives.

**Blue** (*lan*) is not a primary colour in China. It is the colour of the ocean, the sky and immortality. According to legend the universe began as an egg. Out of the egg hatched a man named Pan Gu. Half of Pan Gu's shell became the sky above, and the other half formed the ocean below. Pan Gu grew for 18 000 years, separating the sky from the ocean further and further. Finally he collapsed and became immortal.

**White** (*bai*) is the colour of metal. It corresponds to autumn and the West. White is not a lucky colour for Chinese people.

For thousands of years, white used to be

the colour of mourning and death. When my grandmother died, my sister and I walked behind her coffin wearing white clothes with white ribbons in our hair.

The word *bai* also signifies uselessness and lack of success.

- 'White speech' (*bai hua*) means 'wasted argument'.
- 'White walking' (*bai zou*) means 'a trip taken in vain'.
- 'White arrival' (*bai lai*) means 'useless visit'.
- 'Eat white rice' (*chi bai fan*) means to 'sponge off one's host'.

**Yellow** (*huang*) is the colour of earth. It corresponds to the Centre. Yellow was reserved for the Emperor and members of his imperial family. No commoner was allowed to wear imperial yellow colours, except by permission from the Emperor. To be given a yellow jacket by the Emperor was a mark of special favour.

*Emperor's yellow silk dragon robe, Qing Dynasty*

# THE STORY OF SILK

Legend says that silk was first made by the wife of the Yellow Emperor 5000 years ago. She kept silkworms and invented the loom. Silk fragments, ribbons and threads dating from 3000 BC have been found in eastern China.

Over the years, the Chinese were able to breed a species of silk moth that is blind and unable to fly. Each lays 500 or more eggs in a few days and then dies. After hatching, the baby worms are fed on freshly chopped mulberry leaves day and night for about a month until they become fat. Each then spins a cocoon around itself, and this is where the silk comes from. Every cocoon is made of a filament about 800 metres (875 yards) long.

The cocoons are steamed to kill the worms inside, then they are dipped in hot water to loosen the silk filaments. These filaments are unwound and six to eight filaments are twisted together to make a silk thread. The threads are woven into cloth.

Silk was greatly valued and often used as currency (money). A man's salary would be a certain length of silk per year. Silk garments were worn by Roman emperors, who called the Chinese *Seres* (Silk People). The clothes are beautiful, light and comfortable, being cool in summer and warm in winter.

## SMUGGLED IN STICKS

Because the silk trade was so valuable, Chinese methods of silk production were a closely guarded trade secret. Anyone smuggling silkworm eggs out of China was punished by death.

Around 550 AD, two visiting monks took the risk. They returned from China to the Byzantine Emperor Justin's court with silkworm eggs hidden in their hollow bamboo walking sticks. That was the start of silk production in Constantinople (present-day Istanbul). The Persians learned the art of silk weaving from the Greeks, but it was not until the thirteenth century that silk production became widespread in Italy and the rest of Europe.

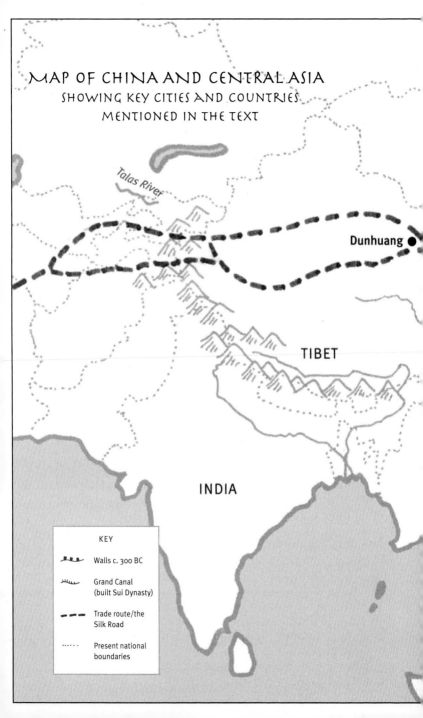

MAP OF CHINA AND CENTRAL ASIA
SHOWING KEY CITIES AND COUNTRIES
MENTIONED IN THE TEXT

Talas River

Dunhuang

TIBET

INDIA

KEY

Walls c. 300 BC

Grand Canal
(built Sui Dynasty)

Trade route/the
Silk Road

Present national
boundaries

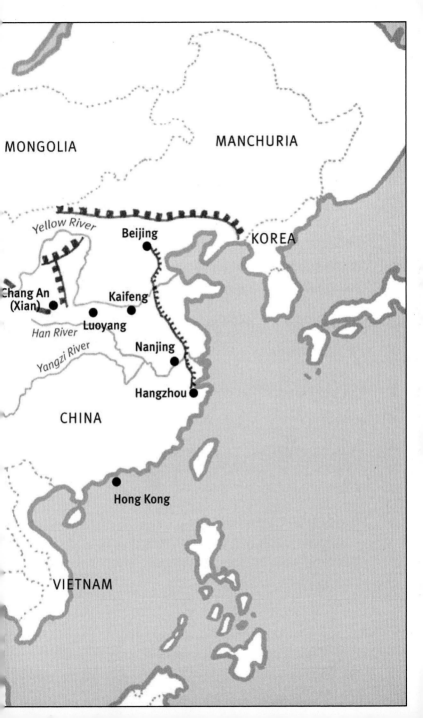

秦

STORY
OF THE
HOUSE
OF
YING

CAPITAL
CITY
XIAN YANG

# FIRST
# EMPEROR
## OF ALL CHINA

259–206 BC

China's written history goes back thousands
of years but we'll begin just 2200 years
ago with the man who first united China.
He began the Great Wall and built the biggest
tomb in history for himself, complete with
an army of 7000 clay soldiers. He said his
Qin Dynasty would last 10 000 generations.
It ended three years after his death.

# BOY-KING WITH A MISSION

The man who became First Emperor, Qin Shi-huang, was just 13 years old when he became ruler of the Kingdom of Qin (pronounced Chin) in central-west China. Although only a boy, he was determined to succeed and to make his mark in history.

When he ascended the throne in 247 BC, China was divided into seven states which had long been at war with one another. The boy-king began his reign with three goals. One was to conquer the other six states and unite the country. Another was to be the most powerful ruler in China. The last was to erect the grandest tomb ever built. He succeeded in all three.

As soon as he became King, he transported 700 000 (seven hundred thousand!) men from all over China to construct a tomb for him just outside his capital city (close to Xian). He really wanted to live for ever and searched for an elixir of immortality but a grand tomb was the next best thing. The project continued until he died 36 years later. It became by far the most elaborate tomb in the world, a complex of many chambers around a central tomb the height of a 25-storey building.

By the time he was 38 years old, he had defeated the six other states and unified the country. He gave himself the title of First Emperor of All China. (The English name 'China' probably came from the word Qin.)

# BUILDING AND BURNING

The First Emperor was a tyrant but also a genius. Besides his tomb, he built the Great Wall and 6500 kilometres (4000 miles) of highways, as well as canals, bridges and palaces. He ordered everyone to use the same coins, weights and measures, and a common written language. Hard-working and disciplined, he read 55 kilograms (120 pounds) of reports written on bamboo slips every day.

Three years before he died the Emperor decided that the

*Qin Shi-huang and his ministers by the Yellow Sea*

history of China was to begin with his reign. He ordered all books written before him to be burned. Any scholar who dared to object was buried alive. In the end, 460 scholars chose to die rather than betray their beloved books. But many more brought their books to the First Emperor out of fear, and the fires burned day and night.

Why was the First Emperor so driven? Some historians believe it was because of his family background. His mother had been the concubine of a rich merchant named Lu before she married the King of Qin. It was widely rumoured that the boy was Lu's son rather than the son of royalty. When the King died, the 13-year-old ascended the throne. He worked day and night to prove that far from being the unworthy son of a mere merchant, he was the greatest king who ever lived.

# TERRACOTTA ARMY

If you go to the Terracotta (clay) Museum in Xian you can view thousands of life-size clay soldiers and horses in battle formation. What an amazing sight!

In 1974, peasants digging for well-water found parts of a terracotta warrior underground. Later digs unearthed many pits around a main tomb, and an enormous number of terracotta soldiers. These had been hidden for over 2000 years. The peasants had found the First Emperor's tomb, now covered by earth and looking like a medium-sized hill among green fields. Recent archeological work shows that the entire tomb complex may be as big as a small town.

In the museum, you'll see row after row of life-sized warriors lined up neatly, ready to do battle on behalf of their master in his afterlife. There are cavalrymen (soldiers on horseback), as well as charioteers standing at attention beside their chariots, holding the reins of their horses. One archer is on one knee, poised to shoot his arrow. You can even see the pattern on the sole of his shoe!

The cavalrymen wear caps with chinstraps, while the officers and charioteers have on more ornate headgear. Their long hair is neatly plaited, pulled on top of the head and tied. Their double-thickness tunics are belted at the waist, with a thick roll of fabric around the neck to prevent chafing from their leather armour. Below the knee, they wear leggings and square-toed shoes.

The average height of these soldiers is 178 centimetres (5 feet 10 inches). Each soldier has a different face. Archeologists think they were modelled on actual soldiers of the First Emperor's imperial guard.

The terracotta army is in one of the smaller tombs. Besides warriors, some of the pits contain life-size clay acrobats, bureaucrats and musicians. But what's in the big one, the Emperor's tomb?

This main tomb has never been opened, but there are stories about it in a book called *Historical Record*, written 2100 years ago by Sima Qian. According to *Historical Record*, there is a huge bronze map of China inside the tomb. It shows the two main rivers of China (Yellow River and the Yangzi River) and on the banks of the rivers are toy carriages and mini palaces. The rivers were filled with mercury, to represent water. There are many other fabulous treasures:

- flocks of animals carved in silver or gold
- plates, lamps and furniture made of jade
- coins
- all kinds of musical instruments
- boxes made of smooth red and black lacquer

- books written on bamboo and silk
- weapons such as swords, lances, halberds, crossbows and arrows.

Above the map, says Sima Qian, there is a huge copper dome showing the sky at night, with the moon and stars traced out in precious jewels.

But why has no one seen the tomb since the Emperor died? One reason is that the whole place is rigged with crossbows, arrows and other dangerous weapons!

First Emperor was buried by his son, the Second Emperor. Second Emperor ordered that all the craftsmen who had installed weapons to protect his father's body must be buried alive in the tomb, so they could never reveal how the booby traps had been set. He also buried alive *all* of his father's concubines (secondary wives) who had not borne any children. Luckily this excluded his own mother.

# DEATH OF THE FIRST EMPEROR

When the First Emperor was 49 years old, he set off on a tour of his empire. Accompanying him were his Prime Minister Li Si, his younger son Prince Hu Hai and the prince's tutor, a eunuch named Zhao Gao. (What's a eunuch? See next page.) He travelled in a chariot pulled by four horses. Fastened to it was an umbrella that could be tilted in any direction to shade him from the sun. (There's a perfect replica, half-size, of this chariot in the Terracotta Museum at Xian.)

Nine months into the tour and far from his capital city, the Emperor became ill and knew he was going to die. He ordered Eunuch Zhao (pronounced Jow) to write to his elder son, Prince Fu Su, and tell him he must hurry to the capital and be ready to bury the Emperor's body in the tomb. At that time, Prince Fu was building the Great Wall in the north with 300 000 troops under his command.

The letter was sealed but not yet given to the messenger when the Emperor died. Eunuch Zhao persuaded Prime Minister Li to destroy the letter. They kept the Emperor's death a secret and began to conspire with his weak-willed younger son, Prince Hu.

They sent a false letter to Prince Fu ordering him to commit suicide. The letter was sealed with the Emperor's seal as if it had come from him. Their messenger rode day and night and arrived at the Great Wall. To prove who he was, he gave Prince Fu the matching half of a tiger tally.

# WHAT IS A EUNUCH?

A eunuch is a man who has had his testicles removed (i.e. he has been castrated). In China, the penis was sometimes removed along with the testicles. The custom started in China during the eighth century BC. Eunuchs were employed as sexless slaves in the ruler's palace to carry out household chores and guard the chastity of his women. In his vast palace, the Emperor was the only 'normal' adult male. He lived there with his wives (sometimes hundreds of them), his children and his eunuchs.

Castration could be a form of punishment but was also a way to get a job in the Emperor's palace. Many men and boys volunteered themselves for castration in order to gain direct access to the royal household. Eunuchs provided personal services such as washing the face, cutting the hair or massaging the feet of the Emperor, his Empress, his concubines and his children, including the future Emperor. Sometimes a prince would gain the throne when still a child. Since he had been looked after by eunuchs all his life, he would often rely heavily on his favourite ones for support and advice.

Eunuchs were supposed to be 'docile, loyal, modest and polite'. The reality could be very different, as we will see from the way Eunuch Zhao behaved.

The tiger tally was a traditional token by which the Emperor transferred his power. Forged in bronze in the shape of a tiger, it had two halves. The right half was kept by the Emperor. The left half was given to the commander at the battlefield. When a messenger's piece fitted the commander's, it proved that his message came directly from the Emperor and must be obeyed at once.

# SOMETHING'S FISHY HERE!

Meanwhile the three conspirators, Prince Hu, Prime Minister Li and Eunuch Zhao, continued touring the country as if the Emperor was still alive. They announced to the attendants that he was unwell and wished to stay in his coach. But the weather grew hot and the corpse began to smell. To hide the odour, Prime Minister Li filled the coach with salted shellfish and spread the word that the Emperor had a sudden craving for preserved abalone! They continued touring until the messenger returned from the Great Wall and reported that Prince Fu was safely dead. Only then did they dare to hurry back to the capital.

Prime Minister Li announced that the First Emperor was dead and Prince Hu was now Second Emperor. Not long afterwards, a power struggle began between Prime Minister Li and the wily eunuch. The Second Emperor sided with his former tutor, Zhao. He had Li executed, and appointed Zhao to be the new prime minister.

Eunuch Zhao was now so powerful that he wished to be the Emperor himself. Only one man stood between him and the throne – the Second Emperor. He decided to test the ministers to see how far they would follow him.

One day, Eunuch Zhao presented a deer to the Second Emperor at court, all the time pointing to the animal and calling it a horse. The Emperor laughed in disbelief and asked the ministers around him for their opinion. Most of them were frightened of the eunuch and said it was a horse. (They were right to be scared – Zhao later punished all those who had dared to call it a deer.) The phrase *pointing to a deer and calling it a horse* has become a well-known proverb in the Chinese language. It describes a situation where right and wrong are deliberately mixed up.

# CHEN SHENG WILL BE KING

One year after the death of the First Emperor, China was in chaos. Rebellious princes and generals turned themselves into warlords and fought for control of the country. However, the first major revolt against the Second Emperor was started not by nobles or commanders, but by two poor peasants from central China named Chen Sheng and Wu Guang.

Chen proclaimed himself to be the reincarnation (reborn person) of Prince Fu Su, come back to life to do battle with his younger brother, the Second Emperor. His followers cut down trees to make weapons, and raised their flags on bamboo poles. Hoisting his flag high above his head, Chen Sheng shouted, 'Kings and generals are made, not born!' (*Hoisting a bamboo pole as a banner of revolt* has become a traditional way of describing any popular revolt against tyranny in China. The phrase was used by the late Communist leader Chairman Mao in the twentieth century.)

Within a month, Chen and Wu's army had swelled to 20 000 infantry (soldiers on foot), 600 chariots and 1000 horsemen. Yet they were no match for the Qin army of 700 000 men. Barely six months later, Chen was murdered by his own carriage driver as he fled east after the defeat of his army.

Chen Sheng's death did not stop other uprisings. Throughout China, many men began revolts of their own, called themselves kings and dreamed of setting up their own dynasties. Among them was a middle-class peasant named Liu Bang, who became founder of the Han Dynasty.

Eunuch Zhao forced the Second Emperor to commit suicide in 207 BC but he himself was murdered by an uncle of the Second Emperor. This uncle was later killed by a powerful warlord who robbed the First Emperor's tomb and torched the terracotta army. The Qin Dynasty came to an end three and a half years after the death of the First Emperor. Altogether it had lasted for only 15 years.

# THE EMPEROR IS THE SON OF HEAVEN

For over 3000 years, the Chinese have believed that the Emperor holds the Mandate of Heaven (*Tian Ming*).

*Tian* means heaven. It's the closest Chinese word to 'God'. *Ming* means life, fate or command.

天命 Thus the term *Tian Ming* has been translated as 'Mandate of Heaven', or 'divine right to rule'.

天子 *Tian Zi* (Son of Heaven) is another term for Emperor.

天下 *Tian Xia* (All under Heaven) means the Emperor's Kingdom.

The Chinese believed that Heaven only supports an Emperor if he is good. Floods, famine, drought or earthquakes will happen if he is bad. Should these natural disasters occur, then it's time to rebel. A successful revolt means that Heaven has passed the Mandate to the new ruler.

Confucius taught that all the land and all the people in China belonged to the Emperor. Army generals and civil ministers must therefore be absolutely loyal to their Emperor because he was the Son of Heaven and had been given the Mandate to Rule. If the Emperor ruled unwisely, however, Heaven would take away his Mandate and give it to somebody else. Natural disasters and famine were signs that the Mandate was about to be taken away from a corrupt ruler. The people would throw him out and the new recipient of Heaven's Mandate would become the next Emperor. This idea continues through Chinese history.

Towards the end of the Han Dynasty in 184 AD, the Yellow Turban Society led a successful rebellion after a series of floods and famine.

In 960 AD, a regiment of disgruntled troops rebelled and founded the Song Dynasty when they were sent to battle on Chinese New Year's Day.

In the mid-fourteenth century, the Yellow River flooded and the Red Turban Society, led by the future First Ming Emperor, drove out the Mongols.

In the early 1900s, the political party that ended the reign of the last Qing Emperor described itself as 'The Association for Changing the Mandate of Heaven'. Many Chinese today believe that the Chinese Communist Party holds the Mandate of Heaven to rule the country.

Just before Chinese New Year in 2008, China suffered its worst snowstorms in 50 years. Over a million people were stranded in railway stations, unable to go home for the festival. Sixty people died and a quarter of a million homes collapsed. Mindful of the close historical connection between 'natural disasters' and 'withdrawal of Heaven's Mandate', President Hu Jintao did his utmost to visit the hardest-hit areas and mobilised the army to bring aid to the victims.

漢

STORY
OF THE
HOUSE
OF LIU

CAPITAL
CITY
CHANG AN

# FOUNDING DYNASTY: THE HAN

206 BC – 220 AD

The Han Dynasty lasted 420 years, and most Chinese people call themselves 'people of Han'. During this period trade began along the route we call 'the Silk Road'. Horses and perfume were brought to China, and traded for silk, tea and porcelain. Cast iron, paper and the seismograph were invented at this time.

# LUCKY LIU

The founder of the Han Dynasty, Liu Bang, was already 48 years old when the First Emperor died. The Liu family were well-off peasants from central China. Liu Bang was handsome, with a 'dragon' (broad) forehead, prominent nose and thick beard. The first time the rich and well-respected magistrate Lu set eyes on Liu Bang he was so impressed that he gave Liu his beloved daughter as his wife.

Generous and big-hearted, Liu Bang was always surrounded by friends. As a young man, he was lazy and refused to do the kind of manual labour that his father and brothers were doing, such as farming and carpentry. He liked wine and women and enjoyed discussing politics with his neighbours.

Finally, at the age of 30, Liu passed the civil service exams and was made chief in a village of a few hundred families. As chief, it was his job to escort convicts to the capital city to work on the First Emperor's palaces and tomb. For about 15 years during the reign of the First Emperor, he travelled often to the capital and saw how the First Emperor lived. 'Ah! This is how a man should live,' he said.

# OUTLAWS

After the death of the First Emperor, rebellions started up all over China. On the way to the capital one day, many of the convicts in Liu Bang's convoy ran away to join the rebels. He was alarmed. According to the law at that time, Liu as chief was responsible for his prisoners, and would be severely punished if anyone escaped. What should he do?

At the next stop, Liu treated his men to wine and drank with them far into the night. Then he said, 'Gentlemen, you are free to go. Since I've already lost so many of you, I can no longer go home. I have no choice but to set you free and become a fugitive myself.'

The men ran off but soon found their path blocked by a large, hissing snake. Terrified, they rushed back and reported to Liu. He calmly took out his sword, strolled over and killed the snake with one stroke. Then he told them again they were free to go.

Most of the men were so impressed that they decided to follow him. They all lived in the wild, hiding from the authorities. More and more joined them. Soon Liu's band numbered several hundred.

# ARROWS OF FORTUNE

At that time, the Magistrate of Pei, Liu's home town, also decided to rebel against the Second Emperor. He soon changed his mind, however, and arrested his fellow plotters, locking the city gates. When Liu Bang returned to the city with his band of followers, the Magistrate denied them entry. Liu then wrote a message on a piece of silk, tied it to an arrow and shot it over the wall. The message was to

*Man on horseback, from Wu-wci, Kansu, Eastern Han Dynasty (bronze)*

the city elders, many of whom had been his wine-drinking friends, and he urged them to lead the people against the corrupt Second Emperor.

The elders took his advice, killed the Magistrate, opened the city gates to Liu Bang and nominated him as the Lord of Pei. Thus a humble man from a peasant family assumed leadership by popular vote in 209 BC.

After the death of the Second Emperor, Liu Bang fought a series of battles (called the Chu-Han Wars) against a powerful warlord from the former Kingdom of Chu. After four years, Liu won and established the Han Dynasty to rule all China, with his capital city at Chang An (now Xian).

The Han Empire stretched from North Korea in the northeast to North Vietnam in the south. To the west, it included mountains and desert north of Tibet.

Trade began to flow between China and the west via the Silk Road. Chinese silk was sold in the markets of Rome. In exchange, the Chinese bought Roman glass, pearls, wool, gold ornaments and perfume.

Liu Bang had grown up as an ordinary peasant. As such, he had a commoner's sense of fair play which made him popular with the average Chinese. He reduced the farm tax from 50 per cent of the crop to 7 per cent and allowed his soldiers to farm part-time. He also chose educated and competent scholars rather than noble aristocrats to run his government. He changed some of First Emperor's harshest laws and allowed his subjects to live in prosperity and peace. (Remember that he didn't have to bear the cost of fighting six other states in order to unite China – First Emperor had done that.)

Liu Bang died in 195 BC from infection of an unhealed arrow wound. He was 61 years old.

## THE CRUEL EMPRESS

Liu Bang's oldest son by his first wife took the throne as Emperor Hui. But the real power was in the hands of Hui's mother, the all-powerful Empress Dowager Lu.

In those days, a man kept as many women as he could afford. Like many men of the time, Liu Bang had a main wife ('big wife') and many concubines ('little wives'). His favourite was Lady Qi (pronounced Chi). Besides being very beautiful, she could sing, dance and play a skilful game of Go – a strategic board game similar to chess. On 4 August every year according to the Chinese calendar, Liu Bang would challenge Lady Qi to a game of Go. She almost always won.

Lady Qi and Liu had a son named Ruyi. For a few

*Jade pendant depicting Fenghuang (Chinese phoenix)*

years before his death, Liu talked of making Ruyi Crown Prince, but he died without doing so.

Empress Lu, Liu's main wife, was jealous of his concubines, especially Lady Qi, but could do nothing while her husband was alive. As soon as he died and her own son was on the throne, she arrested all the women that Liu Bang had been fond of. As for Lady Qi, Empress Lu shaved off her beautiful hair, dressed her in red convict clothes and placed her neck in a square wooden board of such width that she could neither feed herself nor sleep lying down.

The Empress's son, Emperor Hui, was kind and gentle. Fearful that his mother might harm his young half-brother, he invited Ruyi to live with him in his palace. The two brothers ate and slept together. So Empress Dowager Lu was unable to harm one without hurting the other. She secretly kept watch over them, however, and bided her time.

One morning, Emperor Hui decided to go hunting early. He tried to rouse his brother and take him along, but Ruyi was only 12 years old and refused to get up. Since dawn was just breaking, Emperor Hui thought he could safely leave Ruyi for a little while.

*Bronze oil lmap with kneeling servant girl*

As soon as he left his palace, the Empress was informed. She immediately sent an assassin who awoke Ruyi and forced him to drink poisoned wine. When Emperor Hui returned, Ruyi was dead. Mother and son had a furious argument, but there was nothing the Emperor could do to bring the boy back to life. Their quarrel merely sharpened the Empress Dowager's hatred of Ruyi's mother, Lady Qi.

# DARKEST DEEDS

What happened next was truly dreadful. Please jump two paragraphs if you don't like violence. After brooding a while longer, the Dowager Empress gave in to her darkest fantasies. She cut off Lady Qi's hands and feet, blinded her, burned off her ears, sliced off her tongue so she could no longer speak and threw her in a pigsty to grovel in mud and filth among the pigs. Then she gave a party so visitors could come and view the 'human pig'. Among those invited was her son.

At first Emperor Hui did not know what he was seeing. When he finally understood, he was so shocked that he went into a deep depression. He lost all interest in affairs of state and let his mother rule the country.

Emperor Hui died in 188 BC at the age of 22. He had seven young sons by various concubines but no children by his wife. Empress Lu executed the boys' birth mothers after Hui's death so she could have total control over the little princes. One of

Hui's sons became the nominal Emperor but power remained in the hands of Empress Dowager Lu. This boy-emperor was precocious and one day made the remark that when he grew up, he would avenge the death of his real mother. On hearing this, Empress Dowager Lu immediately had him arrested and killed. Next she enthroned another of Hui's sons, with herself as regent. Meanwhile she granted large tracts of land to her own relatives from the Lu family.

Empress Dowager Lu ruled China for another eight years. One day she dreamed that a blue-haired dog ran towards her and bumped her armpit. She awoke in terror and consulted a shaman (a holy man) who advised her to pray for forgiveness because the dog was the spirit of Prince Ruyi, come back to haunt her. The pain in her armpit increased and she died a few weeks later.

After her death in 180 BC, a power struggle developed between Empress Lu's relatives and the sons of Liu Bang's other wives. Helped by the court ministers, the Lius won. They executed many of the Lu clan and eventually placed Liu Bang's fourth son, Prince Dai, on the throne as the next Han Emperor.

# PEOPLE OF HAN

The dynasty Liu Bang began lasted for 400 years and was one of China's greatest. Even today, we Chinese call ourselves 'the people of Han' (*Han Ren*). There is a proverb that says, 'The heart of the people belongs to Han'. This includes all of the following: love of the language, fondness for Chinese food, pride in Chinese culture, reverence for our elders and hope for a better future for China.

Today there are 1.3 billion Han Chinese living in China and overseas. It is the largest single ethnic group in existence. One-fifth of the world's people are Han Chinese. Within China itself, 92 per cent of the people are Han Chinese.

Even outside China, the Han Dynasty is remembered. *Kanji* (Han characters) is a term still used in Japan today for those Chinese characters the Japanese borrowed from China. The Koreans and Vietnamese also adopted Chinese characters in their own written languages.

The first census in recorded history took place during the Han Dynasty. A dictionary was compiled and a university was set up to educate future government ministers in the teachings of Confucius. For 1300 years, success in China depended on passing a set of written examinations based on study of the Confucian classics (see pages 190–1).

So who was this man Confucius who dominated Chinese thinking for so long?

# CONFUCIUS – WOMAN-HATER, FOOD FREAK, RULE-MAKER

Confucius (551–479 BC) was the most famous man in China for 2500 years. His father died when he was three and he was brought up by his mother. As an adult he was impossible to live with. He insisted that every meal be cooked at home and refused to eat anything ready-made from the market. Vegetables not in season were a no-no. If the rice was not white enough or the food was chopped too coarsely, he would push it away. After a few years, his wife had had enough and divorced him. From then on, he disliked all women, calling them 'little people with narrow minds'. He declared that 'Only uneducated women are virtuous.'

Confucius was a teacher, not a prophet or religious leader, nor a writer. He spent the last 13 years of his life travelling from one kingdom to another trying to get a job as a king's adviser. At that time, China was divided into many states at war with one another. His long question-and-answer sessions with his students were written down and published as the *Sayings of Confucius* after his death. He never wrote any books himself.

Confucius taught that to maintain peace and harmony, the son must always respect his father; the father must respect his superior and so on up to the Emperor, who was the Son of Heaven. He said that all the land and all the people in China belonged to the Emperor. Therefore, the minister must always obey his ruler. Not surprisingly, Confucianism was welcomed by Chinese rulers. They recognised the advantage of their officials believing that the Emperor possessed the Mandate to Rule from Heaven.

Confucius also taught that the choice of government officials should depend on *merit* and not birth. How was this done? By a system of written tests or examinations based on Confucian teachings (see pages 190–1).

# SIMA QIAN
## (PRONOUNCED CHIEN)

Sima Qian (145–90 BC) was a writer whose father, Sima Tan, was Grand Historian to the Han Emperor Jingdi. For many years Sima Tan dreamed of writing a history of China from the beginning of time. At his deathbed, the father passed on his collection of documents and historical material to his son, who began to write *Shi-ji* (*Historical Record*). In those days, books were written with a brush and ink on bamboo strips or on pieces of silk. Paper had been invented but was not used for writing until 200 years later.

Sima Qian was a historian in the court of Emperor Wu (156–87 BC), Jingdi's son. Halfway through writing the book, Sima Qian spoke up on behalf of a general who had surrendered to the Xiong Nu (a northern tribe from Mongolia at war with China; also called Huns). The Emperor was outraged and gave Sima Qian the choice of death or castration. Sima Qian chose to be castrated so he could finish his work. In a letter to a friend, he wrote, 'And should my words one day penetrate the minds of readers who will value them . . . then even if I should suffer ten thousand deaths by mutilation, I would have no regrets.'

*Historical Record* is a great work of half a million words divided into 130 chapters. It has been a best-seller in China for the last 2100 years, inspiring the Chinese people to respect their past and love their history. Recent archaeological finds have confirmed over and over again the accuracy of Sima Qian's writing. Many Chinese proverbs used today are direct quotations from stories told in his book. *Pointing to a deer and calling it a horse* is but one example.

*The pages in a bamboo book fold on top of one another in a zig-zag pattern, which means that the entire book can be unfolded into one flat sheet.*

# END OF THE HAN DYNASTY

The Han Dynasty lasted for over 420 years. Gradually, the ruling classes led ever more luxurious and idle lifestyles. They thought only of their own pleasure and paid no heed to the welfare of the people. Within the palace, the court eunuchs gained more and more influence over the Emperor. This led to conflicts with the scholar-officials, who came to despise the eunuchs.

In the last years of the Han Dynasty, there were natural disasters, famine, chaos and peasant rebellions throughout China. Three of the generals appointed by the Emperor to maintain peace carved China into three separate kingdoms, and one of the generals forced the last Han Emperor to abdicate (give up the throne).

The Han Dynasty officially ended in 220 AD.

# THE BEGINNING
## OF THE SILK ROAD

The Silk Road was an ancient trade route connecting China with the Roman Empire.

Emperor Wu, the monarch who castrated historian Sima Qian, sent an envoy, Zhang Qian, to Uzbekistan in Central Asia to look for an ally against the Huns. Zhang was captured by the Huns (and married a Hun wife) before escaping and returning 13 years later.

Emperor Wu was delighted to see him and to learn of countries beyond the land of the Huns. Above all he was delighted by a special breed of fast and powerful horse from Uzbekistan called the 'Heavenly Horse' – so named because the horses appeared to sweat blood and the Chinese thought this was supernatural. They didn't know that this blood came not from sweat glands but from sores caused by parasites growing under the horses' skin.

Six years later, Emperor Wu sent Zhang on a second mission. It was a great success and led to friendly relations between China and Persia (now Iran). For the next 2000 years, goods such as silk, tea and porcelain were taken from China to Central

Asia and Europe. In return, Europe sent glass, amber, wool, linen and perfumes, while Central Asia sent musk, raisins, wine, horses and fur. The goods were sold or bartered from merchant to merchant and town to town before reaching their final destination. There were very few traders who actually travelled the whole distance from one end to another.

The road started from Chang An (Xian – pronounced She-An) in central China and ran west along the Great Wall to the oasis city of Dunhuang on China's north-western border. Dunhuang became known as the Jade Gate to the Silk Road. From there the road went around mountains and through the Asian deserts to the Middle East and Europe.

Trade along the Silk Road flourished during periods of peace, especially the Han Dynasty, the Tang Dynasty and the Yuan (Mongol) Dynasty.

More important than trade was the exchange of ideas and inventions. These were also swapped along the Silk Road from east to west and vice versa. Pilgrims and monks spread Christianity from Rome as well as Judaism and Islam from the Middle East. Buddhism spread from India to China.

Inventions such as the manufacture of silk, paper and printing, gunpowder and the stirrup also travelled on this road along with the camels. Thus another name for the Silk Road could be the Information Superhighway.

# CAST IRON

The Chinese were able to make cast iron from the fourth century BC. One reason was that China had good-quality, heat-resistant clay for making the walls of blast furnaces. The Chinese also knew that by adding phosphorus (which they called 'black earth') to an iron mixture, the iron would melt at a lower temperature, thus requiring less fuel.

During the Han Dynasty, the imperial government took over all cast-iron manufacture. Forty-six foundries were established to make lances, hoes, swords, knives, axes, chisels, saws, pots and pans. Later on, spectacular structures such as pagodas, temples and giant statues were also made. Some of them still survive.

In the second century BC, the Chinese began to make steel and wrought iron by blowing air into melted cast iron over and over again. (We now know that oxygen in the air removes carbon. If much of the carbon is removed from cast iron, the result is steel, which is stronger and harder. If all the carbon is removed from cast iron, you get wrought iron, which is softer and more malleable.) Cast iron was named *raw iron* by the Chinese, steel was called *great iron* and wrought iron was known as *ripe iron*.

The Chinese used cast iron to make ploughs, saws, pots, pans and toys. They used steel to make swords, spears, axes and other weapons. Wrought iron was used for stirrups, bridges and aqueducts.

About 2000 years later, in 1845, the American William Kelly brought four Chinese iron-workers to his factory in Kentucky. They taught him how to make steel by blowing air into molten cast iron to remove carbon. The same method was adopted by British industrialist Sir Henry Bessemer in 1855. Bessemer's process for making steel, invented by the Chinese in the second century BC, is still used today.

# STIRRUPS FOR HORSES

Unlike the nomads of Mongolia and Manchuria, the Chinese did not grow up riding horses. Recognising the superior power of cavalry in warfare, Chinese emperors went to great lengths to buy better breeds of horses from distant kingdoms. To improve their riding skills, the Chinese also invented the metal (iron or bronze) stirrup. They already had the trace harness (fourth century BC) and the collar harness (third century BC). These prevented a horse from being choked when it pulled heavy loads or ploughed the fields.

Iron stirrups provided the rider with a foothold he could use to mount the horse, stabilise himself in the saddle and shoot more accurately with the bow and arrow while galloping. Without stirrups a rider needed to hold on to the horse's mane to avoid falling off.

Metal stirrups were used in China in the third century AD, but did not become common in Europe until 300 years later.

# SEISMOGRAPH

China has been plagued by earthquakes throughout its history. Sima Qian wrote that a powerful earthquake in 780 BC had changed the course of three rivers. The Emperor needed to know where quakes were happening as early as possible in order to assess damage and send help. But how could he find out?

A brilliant court astronomer named Zhang Heng came up with the solution in the second century AD. His seismograph was a large bronze jar with eight dragons arranged in eight different directions. Below the dragons, outside the jar, were eight frogs sitting with their mouths open.

Each dragon held a bronze ball in its mouth. Inside the jar was a thin column that vibrated during an earthquake. There were two round plates with grooves cut in them and a slider that could travel along the grooves. In response to an earth tremor, the slider would move along a groove and push a ball out of a dragon's mouth into the frog's mouth below with a loud clang.

A Han Dynasty historian told the story of a ball falling into a frog's mouth one day even though no tremor had been felt. That frog was on the north-west side of the jar. Several days later, a horseman arrived bringing news of an earthquake that had happened on the same day that the ball had dropped, 650 kilometres (400 miles) away to the north-west.

Unfortunately, the Chinese forgot their own invention. In 1703 AD, the first modern seismograph was designed by a Frenchman.

Besides inventing the seismograph, Zhang Heng also invented the 'south-pointing carriage' and the odometer.

The *south-pointing carriage* was shaped like a wheeled chariot. It had a jade figure on top whose right arm always pointed south no matter which way the chariot turned. The mechanism did not involve a magnetic compass but worked via a train of differential gears, rather like a modern car.

The *odometer* was called a '*li*-counting drum-carriage'. A mechanical wooden figure sitting on the carriage would strike a drum after the wheel had turned enough to have traversed a *li* (500 metres, or 550 yards).

# AGE OF DISUNION

## 220–589 AD

For hundreds of years after the Han Dynasty, generals and warlords fought one another to seize control of China. Because of all the fighting, this period is called the Age of Disunion.

After the collapse of the Han Dynasty, many non-Han tribes from beyond the Great Wall invaded China and seized power for themselves. The most successful were the Tuoba Xianbei, a northern nomadic tribe travelling between Manchuria and Mongolia. They settled in China, married Chinese people, adopted Chinese culture and converted to Buddhism. (If you go to the Longmen Caves in Luoyang, you can see over 100 000 rock-cut Buddha sculptures carved by these immigrants. Some statues are over 10 metres high.)

During the fifth century, millions of people packed up

and moved south across the Yangzi River to escape the disorder in the north. They set up a prince in a separate capital in Jiankang (present-day Nanjing). China became divided into north and south.

Famine, banditry and strife continued. Warlords fought one another for control across the land. Many soldiers rebelled against their own generals. Civil war broke out as those sent to fight the rebels declared their independence and proclaimed themselves kings. Because of all the fighting and uncertainty, many people turned to Buddhism or Daoism for solace during the Age of Disunion.

*Eastern Wu jar, 222–280 AD*

In 577 the northern rulers, the Zhou (pronounced Jo), finally conquered the southern states and unified China. Four years later, a Xianbei general killed all the Zhou princes and established the Sui Dynasty.

The history of these centuries of upheaval has been miraculously preserved in some amazing caves near Dunhuang, in north-western China. Examination of the caves and their contents is like taking a stroll through ancient China. You can read more about the discovery of this extraordinary cave art on pages 203–5.

# ALL THE ISMS IN CHINA: CONFUCIANISM, DAOISM, BUDDHISM

There's a saying that every Chinese wears a Confucian thinking cap, a Daoist robe and Buddhist sandals.

**CONFUCIUS** (551–479 BC) was a philosopher, but not a prophet. Hence Confucianism was a way of life, not a religion. Confucius taught that respect for parents was the root of virtue. He never denied the possibility of life after death or the existence of spirits. When questioned directly, however, he answered, 'Respect the spirits, but keep them at a distance.' He also said, 'Not know life, how know death?'

**DAOISM** (or Taoism) was based on the writings of two ancient philosophers, Lao Zi and Zhuang Zi. In Daoism, the goal is spiritual freedom. This is to be achieved in the realm of Nature. Following Nature means taking no action. Man should see his life cycle as part of Nature and accept change as the *dao* (way) of everything in the universe.

**BUDDHISM** was a religion that came to China from India during the Han Dynasty. Buddhists believe that the life we live now is not the only life, but one of a great series of

lives that extends far back into the past and stretches into future lives until we attain enlightenment. The balance of good and bad deeds in our present life determines our fate in our next life. If we are bad, then we might be reborn (reincarnated) as an animal or an insect. If we are very, very good, then our souls will be absorbed into the supreme soul of the universe and we will be permanently released from the ceaseless round of rebirths, deaths and suffering.

# CAVES OF A THOUSAND BUDDHAS

The Mogao Caves are set into a sheer wall of the Echoing Sand Mountain, at the edge of the Dunes of the Singing Sands, Dunhuang. They are not natural caves but a honeycomb of grottoes carved into the rock. They contain 2400 Buddhist statues and wall after wall of paintings dating from the fourth century to the fourteenth.

A book written during the Tang Dynasty claims that Yuezun, a Buddhist monk, created the Mogao Cave temples in 366 AD. In a dream, he saw golden sunrays reflecting from a mountain peak and shining on him, dancing and shimmering like a thousand Buddhas. When he woke, Yuezun was so inspired he persuaded a wealthy pilgrim to pay for the building of the first 'cave-temple' at Dunhuang. On its walls he painted a mural. Other Buddhist monks followed, creating more temples (in the end there were 492) and more murals.

Because the caves are dark and dry, the paintings have kept their original rich colours. Most of them depict traditional Chinese stories. Some murals illustrate *sutras* (Buddhist teachings). There are also religious texts written in Chinese, Turkic, Uigur, Tibetan and Mongolian.

# PAPER

Recently, a Han Dynasty postal station was discovered not far from Dunhuang. Excavations unearthed over 17 000 relics. Besides wooden and bamboo slips bearing military messages, archaeologists found pieces of paper, dating back to 94 BC.

Paper made from hemp (marijuana plant) dating back even earlier, to the second century BC, has been discovered in a tomb near Xian. Paper in those days was thick and coarse. It was not used for writing but was made (like cloth) into wraps, hats, jackets, shoes, blankets and armour.

In 105 AD, during the Han Dynasty, a palace eunuch named Cai Lun invented a way to make thinner paper for writing. He found that if he boiled plant fibres (pulp from the bark of mulberry trees, hemp, rags, old fishing nets) in water, he would end up with a soupy pulp. The fibres would gradually stick back together and form a mat. After draining off the excess water with a screen and allowing the mats to stiffen, he ended up with sheets of paper which could be peeled off and dried.

From then on, people used paper instead of silk or strips of bamboo for writing in China. Today, Cai Lun is honoured in China and Japan as the patron of paper-making.

The Chinese adapted paper for many other uses such as paper handkerchiefs to wipe the nose (first century BC), toilet paper (sixth century AD), newsletters (740 AD), printed books (ninth century AD), playing cards (ninth century AD) and paper money, also called 'flying money' (ninth century AD).

In 751 AD, the Chinese army lost a battle against the Arabs along the Talas River. During the turmoil, the Arabs captured a caravan of Chinese craftsmen skilled in the art of making paper. They were brought to Samarkand in Uzbekistan as prisoners of war. Their captors made them set up a paper factory in their new country. Some years later, Harun al-Rashid (the famous caliph associated with the book *Arabian Nights*) brought a few Chinese craftsmen to Baghdad and founded a paper mill there in 794 AD. Still later, the Arabs transferred the technology to Egypt, North Africa and (in the twelfth century) Spain, Italy and France.

# MATCHES

In 577 AD, a group of court ladies in the northern city of Yeh (now called Lin-chang) ran out of tinder to start a fire and found themselves unable to cook. Starving and desperate, they came up with the idea of covering the tips of little sticks of pinewood with sulphur. Striking such a stick against a hard surface would bring a little flame like an ear of corn, according to a book written in the tenth century. The book also reported that these little sticks were first called 'light-bringing slaves'. Later they were renamed 'fire inch-sticks' and sold in the marketplace. Matches are still called 'firesticks' in China today.

Matches appeared in Europe in 1530. They might have been brought to Italy by Marco Polo. A Chinese book published in 1270 AD reported that matches were being sold in the street markets of Hangzhou, a city that Marco visited and admired.

What happened to the ladies who invented the matches? Unfortunately, they were all killed when the Sui Dynasty was established.

唐

STORY
OF THE
HOUSE
OF LI

CAPITAL
CITY
CHANG AN

# GOLDEN DYNASTY: THE TANG

589–907 AD

Tang emperors controlled huge territories.
Foreigners, students and pilgrims
flocked to the capital. Poetry and art
flourished. The first and only woman
Emperor reigned during this period, and
the world's first book was produced.

Many historians consider the short-lived Sui Dynasty to be part of the Tang Dynasty. The Sui lasted only 36 years and the second and last Sui Emperor was cousin to the first Tang Emperor. Their mothers were sisters.

## BLOOD AND BUDDHISM?

It seems very strange that Buddhism, which preaches peace, should give rise by violence to a new kingdom. But that is just what happened in 581 AD, when a general named Yang Jian established the Sui Dynasty in the name of Buddhism.

Yang came from an aristocratic family. His forebears were part Xianbei (from Mongolia and Manchuria) and part Chinese. An ancestor was Prime Minister to a Han Dynasty emperor. His father, grandfather, great-grandfather and great-great-grandfather were all army generals or governors.

Yang was married at 16 to the 13-year-old daughter of his commanding officer. He loved her greatly and swore to be faithful, an act of loyalty that was highly unusual for a man of that era. He and his wife were both Buddhists.

One of their daughters became the wife of the King of Zhou (a short-lived dynasty in north China), and Yang served as his Prime Minister. When the King of Zhou died, Yang's daughter rose to be Empress Dowager to her stepson, the Crown Prince. Prime Minister Yang stepped in and took the throne by force. After killing all 59 (fifty-nine!) Zhou princes, he took another eight years to conquer the south and unite the country, thus ending almost 400 years of strife between rival rulers. He then razed the southern capital of Nanjing and forced the nobles living there to move to Chang An.

How did he justify killing all those people? It seems he saw himself as a Buddhist knight who would, if necessary, use force to defend and spread the Buddhist faith. In spite of the bloody way he seized power, he named himself Wendi, or 'Cultured Emperor'.

Wendi ruled China for 23 years. He referred to himself as a Disciple of Buddha and proclaimed that all his subjects should become enlightened through Buddhism and lead happy lives. He erected Buddhist monuments throughout his kingdom and sent out monks to display sacred relics and preach about Buddhist texts. He re-introduced the Han system of examinations for government jobs so that people were appointed according to merit, not birth. He assigned farm land to the peasants, giving more land to people with more children. He lowered taxes and built a network of waterways to ease the transport of grain by boat.

It was a time of prosperity not seen since the Han Dynasty. In 592 AD, eleven years into Wendi's reign, his storehouses were overflowing with food and silk. The nation was peaceful and prosperous. People whispered that Wendi was indeed the rightful recipient of the Mandate of Heaven (see pages 30–1).

Wendi became famous for having only two concubines, the smallest number of concubines among Chinese emperors of that era. It was even rumoured that he did not have sex with either of his concubines while his first wife was alive. (Wendi remains one of the very few emperors in Chinese history to have led such a lifestyle.)

# HANDSOME, BUT AN UGLY CUSTOMER

Wendi had five sons. The second, Yangdi, was good-looking and capable but also devious. Yangdi helped his father conquer the Chen Dynasty to the south and unite China. For this achievement, he was highly praised, and his chief general was made Prime Minister.

Being the second son, Yangdi was not supposed to inherit the throne. Yangdi and the prime minister began plotting against the Crown Prince, Yangdi's older brother. They accused him of spending too much money and having too many concubines. (Meanwhile, Yangdi kept his many affairs secret and forced his concubines to have abortions if they became pregnant.)

The two also spread a false rumour that the Crown Prince was planning treason against Wendi and intending to kill

Yangdi. Wendi believed the rumours. He deposed the Crown Prince and put him under house arrest, making Yangdi Crown Prince instead. Yangdi made sure his brother never saw their parents again.

# DEATH OF WENDI

In 602 AD, the Empress died. The Emperor was grief-stricken. Yangdi pretended to mourn his mother and refused to eat in front of his father, but in private he dined normally.

Two years later, Emperor Wendi became very ill. Around this time Yangdi tried to rape his father's favourite concubine, Consort Chen. Distressed, she told the Emperor. He pounded the bed and shouted, 'Disgusting animal! How can I trust him after this! His mother spoiled him. He will destroy me!' He summoned his Minister of Defence and another high official and ordered them to get his son. They were about to call Yangdi when the Emperor added, 'Not him! My oldest son!' The two ministers left to do his bidding.

Meanwhile, the Prime Minister reported the news to Yangdi. The two friends sprang into action. First they forged the Emperor's seal on an edict to arrest the two ministers and put them in jail. Next they replaced the Emperor's guards at the Summer Palace with Yangdi's guards. From then on, only men loyal to Yangdi were allowed to enter the Emperor's palace or attend to his needs. All the ladies-in-waiting and eunuchs were expelled. Soon after, the Emperor died.

Yangdi immediately took Wendi's two concubines as his own. As the new Emperor, he promoted his friend the Prime Minister, exiled the two ministers who had been at his father's bedside, and executed his oldest brother. Three years later, he killed that brother's eight young sons.

# GRAND DREAMS, MANY DEATHS

Emperor Yangdi reigned for 13 years, between 604 and 617 AD. He was a man of grandiose ideas. He conscripted an enormous labour force of millions of workers. When told there were not enough men, he started conscripting women as well. Besides erecting massive imperial palaces at both Chang An (western capital) and Luoyang (eastern capital), his workers extended the Great Wall and built hundreds of kilometres of imperial highways. He also ordered them to put up 40 secondary palaces around the empire so he could have places to rest on his occasional tours of the provinces. Finally, he built the 2000-kilometre (1200-mile) Grand Canal which linked the Yangzi River in the south to the Yellow River in the north. Even today, the Chinese Grand Canal is still the longest artificial river in the world.

The project was finished in only five months but the death toll was horrific. Nearly half of the millions of labourers conscripted to build Yangdi's projects died of exhaustion from overwork, lack of food or disease.

Yangdi celebrated the opening of the Grand Canal by sending a fleet of elaborately carved barges called Dragon Boats down the waterway. These barges were pulled by an army of servants dressed in red, blue and green silk brocade. The procession went on for nearly 100 kilometres (60 miles).

To relieve his boredom one grey and freezing winter's day, he forced thousands of women to make colourful paper and silk flowers, then go out into the icy streets and stick the blossoms on to the bare branches to 'improve the view'.

Meanwhile, never thinking of the hardship he was imposing on his subjects, Yangdi also ordered various military campaigns against his neighbours. Thousands of his soldiers died of malaria when he led the army into Vietnam. But the most disastrous were his four failed expeditions against Korea. According to official records, out of 300 000 Chinese soldiers who went to attack Korea during one campaign, only 2700 returned to China. The other 297 300 died.

## THINGS FALL APART

Rebellion broke out among the peasants. To avoid military duty, men and boys would deliberately break their legs or arms. They called their injured limbs 'lucky feet' or 'auspicious hands'! Many of Yangdi's own generals rose up against him. Yangdi became especially alarmed when 20 generals did not send greetings to him at the Chinese New Year imperial celebration in 616 AD. This was a clear signal that they were about to rebel.

He escaped south down his own Grand Canal in 616 AD with the best of his troops. As soon as he left, rebel armies captured his biggest granaries and invaded his two northern capital cities. Li Yuan, an army general and Yangdi's first cousin, occupied the north-west and declared Yangdi's grandson the new child Emperor of Sui with himself as regent. He also gave Yangdi the new title of 'Retired Emperor'!

Meanwhile, Yangdi was doing his best to forget his troubles, living a life of luxury in a new palace with over 100 fine suites, each hosted by a beautiful maiden. He and his Empress and favourite concubines would dine in a different suite each evening.

The troops he had brought with him were all from the north. They began to realise that Yangdi had no intention of ever returning. Missing their families and uncertain of their future, they began to desert.

In 618 AD, the commander of the imperial guards, General Yuwen Huaji, led his officers and men into the royal palace and cornered Yangdi, accusing him of misdeeds. He had one of Yangdi's sons executed to show he was serious. Yangdi offered to take poison but no poison could be found. He then took off his scarf and pointed to his neck. One of the soldiers stepped forward and strangled him with it.

Afterwards the rebels killed a number of high-level officials and relatives of Yangdi but spared the lives of the women, including his Empress and consorts. With no one to help her, the Empress made caskets for her husband and son out of the headboards from their beds.

As soon as news of Yangdi's death reached the capital city of Chang An, Li Yuan removed Yangdi's grandson from the throne and declared himself the 'Imperial Founder' and First Emperor of the Tang Dynasty on 18 June 618 AD. Four years later, after uniting China, Li Yuan reburied Yangdi with the proper honours due to an Emperor.

## TANG TRIUMPHS

Li Yuan, founder of the Tang Dynasty, was an aristocrat. He was a nephew of Wendi, the first Sui Emperor, and was a provincial governor during Wendi's reign. Yangdi (his first cousin) promoted him to be a general.

Li Yuan inherited the accomplishments of the two Sui emperors, including the two capital cities Chang An and Luoyang, the Grand Canal and the Great Wall. Copying Wendi, he set up six ministries to run personnel, finance, army, justice, public works and rites. He tried to distribute land equally among his people, lowered taxes and further refined the examination system. He welcomed visitors from foreign countries and their ideas. The result was a dynamic, prosperous and cosmopolitan society.

# A TALE OF THREE SONS

Li Yuan was a widower with three sons by his dead wife Duchess Dou. (There were other sons by his concubines.) According to tradition, he appointed his oldest son as the Crown Prince. The Crown Prince was capable, but he was overshadowed by his younger brother, the Second Prince, a natural leader and commander of troops since the age of 18. The Second Prince had defeated four of Tang's most dangerous rivals on his father's climb to the throne. The Third Prince was especially close to the Crown Prince.

The Emperor gave his sons equal and complete powers, and an order from any of the three carried the same weight as one from the Emperor himself. Yet they were endlessly jealous of each other. Third Prince even talked of assassinating Second

Prince at a dinner in the Crown Prince's palace, but the Crown Prince said no.

One of the Crown Prince's army commanders had a quarrel with the Crown Prince and rebelled. The Emperor was furious. He sent Second Prince to subdue the uprising and offered to make him Crown Prince in place of his older brother if he succeeded. However, the Emperor's concubines and youngest son objected. So, on Second Prince's return after subduing the mutiny, the Emperor did not depose the Crown Prince.

In the summer of 626, an army from a north-western province attacked Tang troops. Instead of sending Second Prince, the Emperor told his third son to deal with the invaders. He also transferred some of Second Prince's troops to Third Prince for the battle. Fearful that his younger brother would deplete his army and harm him, Second Prince decided to strike first.

## TWO HEADS ON ONE LANCE

On the night of 1 July 626, Second Prince wrote to his father, accusing his two brothers of having affairs with the Emperor's concubines. He went to his father's palace at the crack of dawn on 2 July and posted his guards at the north gate. Meanwhile, the concubines learned of his accusations and warned his two brothers by messenger.

When they heard the news of their brother's accusation, the first and third princes rode to the palace on horseback. As they approached the gate, they sensed that something was wrong. Alarmed, they turned around to gallop home. Second Prince pursued them, shouting, 'Wait! Big Brother!' The Third Prince fired three arrows at him but missed. Second Prince, who was an expert archer, then fired a single arrow at the Crown Prince, killing him.

The horses began to panic. Third Prince fell off his mount. Meanwhile, Second Prince's mare galloped into the forest and threw him to the ground so violently that he was unable to get up. Third Prince sprang on top of him and tried to strangle him with his bow. At this moment, the captain of Second Prince's guards arrived with 70 men. The captain shot Third Prince with an arrow and killed him.

Back at the northern gate, the Crown Prince's guards had arrived and were battling Second Prince's troops. Just at that moment, Second Prince's captain galloped up with the heads of the murdered Crown Prince and his brother, Third Prince. At the sight of their masters' heads mounted on the captain's lance, the men fled.

Second Prince now ordered his captain to enter the palace with his men. They advanced all the way into the Emperor's inner chamber. The captain knelt in front of the monarch and said, 'The Crown Prince and Third Prince have committed treason. Second Prince had to execute them. He is concerned about Your Majesty and sent me here to protect you.'

# CHANGE OF TUNE

The Emperor consulted his ministers. They advised that he should go along with his remaining son to placate him. The Emperor therefore summoned Second Prince to his chamber and the son knelt in front of his father and wept. Even so, Second Prince insisted that all the sons of his two brothers be executed, though he did pardon his brothers' guards. Three days later, the Emperor named him Crown Prince and ruler. In September, the Emperor abdicated. His son ascended the throne as Taizong, Second Emperor of the Tang Dynasty.

# MODEL RULER

Taizong's armies defeated Korea, pushed into North Vietnam and ended up controlling most of Central Asia. He turned out to be an able administrator and benevolent ruler. He had a new legal code written which became the model for all later dynasties. Afterwards, it was even adopted by Japan, Korea and Vietnam. He made sure his soldiers learned how to farm the land, and let them alternate between the farm and the fighting frontier. He established the Equal Field System under which every person was given one-third of a hectare (1 acre) to farm. At their death, the land would go back to the state. He proclaimed that although all land was owned by the Emperor, every person was entitled to farm a piece of it.

Many Chinese consider him to be one of the greatest emperors who ever lived. His reign was taken as a standard against which all others were compared. He tried hard not to abuse his power and often criticised the last Sui Emperor Yangdi for his extravagance and tyranny. He surrounded himself with capable ministers and listened to their criticism and advice. During his reign, the Tang Dynasty entered a golden age in art, culture, calligraphy, literature and poetry.

Eleven years after he ascended the throne, the Second Emperor took a 14-year-old girl as one of his concubines. (In those days, the Emperor kept hundreds of concubines.) Her name was Wu Zetian. He did not know it, but after his death, Wu Zetian would become the only woman Emperor (not just Empress) in the history of China.

# EMPRESS WU

Wu Zetian (625–705 AD) was born into a rich and aristocratic family. As a child, she was taught to read and write. Noting her intelligence after she became his concubine, the Second Emperor made her his secretary. During the next 12 years, she drafted policies and advised the Emperor and his ninth son, Crown Prince Li Zhi, on foreign affairs. The Crown Prince was a timid, kind young man, only three years younger than his stepmother. Over the years, both the Second Emperor and the Crown Prince came to rely on Wu Zetian for advice.

### THE EMPEROR AND THE NUN

The Second Emperor died in 649 AD. As was the custom, all his concubines were sent to a Buddhist nunnery after his death. Meanwhile, the Crown Prince took the throne and the name of Gaozong, Third Emperor of the Tang Dynasty. He continued to consult his stepmother in the nunnery and eventually took her back to his palace as his concubine. This caused a scandal but since the Emperor was the Son of Heaven, he could do as he wished.

*Emperor Gaozong*

Six years later, Wu Zetian's baby daughter died. No one knew why. The baby's death was blamed on the Third Emperor's two favourite women in the palace: his main wife, Empress Wang, and a concubine, Xiao. There's a story that Wu Zetian persuaded the Third Emperor to cut off the two women's arms and legs, then drown them in a large vat of wine. After their execution, the Third Emperor promoted Wu Zetian from concubine to Empress.

## POWER BEHIND THE SCREEN

Eleven years into his reign, Emperor Gaozong suffered a series of strokes and could no longer speak. From that time until he died 23 years later, Empress Wu ruled China from behind a screen placed next to the throne. Sometimes the speechless Third Emperor sat on the throne, but more often than not the throne was empty. After he died in 683, she reigned for seven years in the name of her two sons, favouring one and then the other. In 690, she deposed her sons, proclaimed herself Emperor of Zhou and took over the throne. During the thousands of years of imperial Chinese history, Empress Wu was the only woman Emperor.

Confucius, who despised women, had proclaimed that 'Keeping a woman on the throne is as unnatural as having a hen crow like a rooster at dawn.' Empress Wu defied Confucian teaching and the strong opposition of her ministers by forming her own secret police. She reigned as Emperor for 15 years, until 705 AD.

During Empress Wu's reign, women were allowed to be financially independent and to be educated in philosophy, politics and ethics. Divorce was permitted and girls were taught to read and write. This was a tremendous gain because Confucius had declared that 'only uneducated women are virtuous'. In fact, many Confucian parents deliberately did not educate their daughters.

Empress Wu and her family practised Buddhism, which flourished during her reign. She rebuilt and added to the Giant Wild Goose Pagoda (built 652 AD).

Empress Wu published farming manuals to help farmers and introduced labour-saving devices in agriculture. She reduced taxes and allowed the peasants to keep a larger share of their produce for themselves. She chose her ministers for their talent alone, not for their birth, family connections or gender. Her palace secretary was a woman poet. The Empress listened to her critics and rewarded those who gave good advice.

When she was 80 years old, Empress Wu was deposed by her oldest son in a palace coup arranged by that son's wife, the future Empress Wei. In 705, male rule of the Tang Dynasty was re-established under the Fourth Emperor. (Empress Wu's reign did not count in the numbering system.) She died nine months later and was buried at Chang An next to her stepson/husband, the Third Emperor Gaozong. She chose as her gravestone a plain slab without an epitaph. Wilful to the end, she said she wanted to be judged by future generations on her merits alone.

# THE WOMEN FIGHT IT OUT

The Fourth Emperor was a weak and easy-going man completely under the control of the women in his life. He ruled China for five years (or his wife did) and died in 710 AD, supposedly poisoned by her. After his death, there was a power struggle between his widow and his sister. Eventually, both were killed and the Fourth Emperor's younger brother took the throne as the Fifth Emperor. He abdicated to make way for his third son, who became the Sixth Emperor two years later.

# PINNACLE

Sixth Emperor Xuanzong reigned from 712 to 756. His was the longest reign of the Tang Dynasty. During the first 28 years, China reached a pinnacle of greatness that has not been equalled since. Then he fell in love with a beautiful younger woman at the age of 55. From then on for 16 years, he was under her spell, neglected his duties and finally came to a disastrous end.

He was an outstanding ruler until 740 AD. He employed competent ministers, registered the entire population, improved tax collection, repaired the Grand Canal and reopened the Silk Road. The Tang army was able to subdue

*Zhang Guo having an audience with Emperor Xuanzong (Yuan Dynasty painting)*

the nomads from Central Asia, Manchuria, Korea, Tibet and Mongolia. The city of Chang An was then the biggest and most cosmopolitan city in the world. There were two million residents and even a newsletter in 740, according to some sources. The total population of the country rose to over 50 million people. At this point, China was the most powerful nation on earth.

The Tang emperors inherited the enormous palaces erected during the Sui Dynasty, including the two capitals Chang An and Luoyang. Foreigners flocked to pay tribute to the Emperor at his magnificent court. They and their ideas were warmly welcomed. Chang An became known as

the centre of an international community. Persians, Turks, Arabs, Tibetans and Mongolians arrived from the West via the Silk Road. Others came from Japan, Korea, India and Vietnam. Poetry, music and dancing flourished.

Woodblock printing became popular during Sixth Emperor's reign and he was known as a patron of the arts. Li Bai and Du Fu, two of China's greatest poets, lived and wrote at this time. The elegant simplicity of Tang poetry, architecture, calligraphy and ceramics made this truly the golden age of Chinese civilisation.

At Dunhuang, you can see 220 caves carved and decorated during the Tang Dynasty. Wall paintings show

*Tang court playing polo*

the people at work and play: musicians, acrobats, dancers, men and women on horseback, foreign merchants and ladies playing *cuju* football (similar to soccer and invented in the Han Dynasty). Other outdoor sports included archery, horse polo, cockfighting and tug of war.

## GOING DOWNHILL

Everything changed when the Sixth Emperor's favourite consort died in 737 AD. The Emperor was much saddened and yearned for a new love. His palace eunuch Gao finally found a replacement in Yang Guifei, a 22-year-old beauty who was at that time already married to one of the Emperor's own sons (his eighteenth!). Many Chinese historians believe that the fate of the Tang Dynasty would have been entirely different if Yang Guifei had not been so beautiful – if she'd had a bigger nose or smaller eyes.

His Majesty fell in love with her straight away and declared he must have her. To avoid a scandal, he made her divorce her husband and enter a Daoist nunnery for two years. At the end of that period, his son was given a new wife. The Emperor rebuilt a palace complete with hot springs for Yang and made her his imperial consort of the highest rank.

Unable to deny Yang anything, the Emperor showered favours on her and her relatives. Lychees being her favourite fruit, he had them delivered by imperial messengers riding fast horses in relays day and night so she could satisfy her craving. Two men of Consort Yang's family were permitted to marry two princesses from the royal family. Her sisters were given titles and money. Her first cousin became a high-ranking official, eventually the Emperor's Prime Minister. Her favourite court jester, a Turkish army officer by the name of An Lushan, became her 'adopted son', and was later promoted to be commander in charge of 164 000 troops patrolling the border around Beijing.

The Emperor paid less and less attention to affairs of state, leaving the day-to-day administration to Prime Minister Li Linfu. Seeing the Emperor

*The beautiful Yang Guifei*

mesmerised by his beautiful concubine, Li set out to seize more and more power. He appointed non-Han military officers such as An Lushan as commanders at the front, thinking they would be less likely to compete with him in the Emperor's court. To lessen his workload, he gave the military commanders total control over their own troops.

# DEFEAT ON THE TALAS RIVER

In 751, a power struggle arose between tribal rulers in central Asia (now Kazakhstan). One side asked for help from the Arab Muslims in Baghdad, the other requested assistance from Tang China. After battling for five days, the Chinese army was soundly defeated by the Arabs on the banks of the Talas River.

Chinese historians barely mention this battle, considering it to be a minor border skirmish. Western historians, however, believe it to be a key event. Tang China never regained its prestige and dominance in central and west Asia after this defeat. The Arab victory helped the spread of Islam throughout Central Asia.

There was one unexpected result of the battle at Talas River – the Arabs learned the secret of paper-making (see pages 61–2). In the long run, this may have been as important as the military victory.

# REVOLT OF AN LUSHAN

With an enormous army under his control and no oversight from the Sixth Emperor, An Lushan decided to revolt. (Remember, he was the former court jester and Consort Yang's adopted son.) He made his preparations carefully and bided his time.

In 752, Prime Minister Li died and was replaced by Consort Yang's cousin, Yang Guozhong. The distracted Emperor said nothing, even when Prime Minister Yang dug up Li's body, 'exccuted' him for treason although he was already dead, and 'confiscated' Li's enormous estate for himself.

Three years later, An Lushan concluded that his time had come. In 755, he declared that he was raising the banner of revolt against the corrupt Prime Minister Yang. He ordered his troops to sail down the Grand Canal towards the imperial capital Chang An, and promised to treat all who surrendered with the utmost respect. More and more soldiers and peasants joined him. In less than a year, he had captured Luoyang. There he declared himself Emperor of the Great Yan Dynasty and moved towards Chang An (which he was to capture six months later).

# NO ESCAPE

Terrified, the Emperor took his consort and prime minister and escaped south. Along the way, at a small relay station, the imperial guards mutinied. At first they demanded the execution of Prime Minister Yang. After he was killed, they insisted on the death of the Emperor's consort. Unable to carry out the deed, the Emperor buried his face in his hands. The consort took the sash from her robe and hanged herself. She was 38 years old.

Heartbroken, the Sixth Emperor abdicated in favour of his son, who took up the defence of Tang against the rebels. The old man died a few years later, at the age of 77, still mourning his beloved concubine.

*Emperor Xuanzong fleeing Chang An*

An Lushan, who had become increasingly obese and paranoid, was killed by his own son, who in turn was killed by his own general. The rebellion dragged on for a total of eight years and finally ended in 763. The death toll was estimated to be 36 million, the highest for any war until World War II, 1200 years later.

The Tang Dynasty never recovered its former prestige and glory. The empire dissolved into an assortment of local regimes, each headed by its own commander. They were allowed to raise their own troops, collect their own taxes and even to pass on their title. For the next 150 years, the Emperor was merely a figurehead.

The official end of the Tang Dynasty came in 906 AD when the last Tang Emperor was forced to abdicate his throne in favour of one of his rebellious military governors. There followed a chaotic period of temporary regimes and warlords called the Period of Five Dynasties and Ten Kingdoms. In 960 AD, a military officer named Zhao (pronounced Jow) seized control and founded the Song Dynasty.

# PRINTING

Block printing was invented during the Tang Dynasty, around 710 AD. A calligrapher (expert in handwriting) would copy words onto a sheet of paper with brush and ink. This paper was glued face down onto a block of fruit wood, usually pear wood. The words could be seen through the paper but were reversed. Carvers chipped away the wood between the characters. The wood-block now had mirror images of Chinese words raised up like those on a seal or rubber stamp. Ink was spread on the wood, paper (or silk) laid on top and the ink then rubbed into the paper (or silk) with a pad. Hundreds, if not thousands, of copies were printed from the same woodblock in a short time. A book would require many different blocks but these printing blocks could be stored for long periods.

The earliest printed text that exists is a Buddhist scroll printed in China during the eighth century AD. The oldest printed *book* in the world is the Buddhist *Diamond Sutra* printed in the year 868 AD.

Besides printing in black and white, the Chinese also invented colour printing. During the Song Dynasty, paper money was printed in three colours to prevent counterfeiting. Calendars, Buddhist texts, playing cards and pictures of goddesses or pagodas on silk were also printed in large numbers.

Movable type was invented in 1041 (Song Dynasty) by a printer named Bi Sheng. He cut Chinese characters out of sticky clay and baked them in an oven to harden them. These were kept in wooden cases, clearly labelled. In printing a document, he 'glued' the characters onto an iron tray filled with a mixture of wax and pine sap. A full tray resembled a wooden printing block. When the printing was finished, he melted the wax and put away the clay characters until he needed them again. Later, it became more common to make movable type out of wood or metal.

The Mongols introduced movable wooden type from China into Persia, which was conquered by the brother of Kublai Khan, First Emperor of the Yuan Dynasty. Paper money (called *chao* in Chinese) began to be printed in Persia in 1294. The word *chao* entered the Persian language and banknotes are still called *chao* in Iran, even today. The Mongols also conquered Russia in 1240, Poland in 1259 and Hungary in 1283. Block printing appeared in all three countries as well as the rest of Europe during the fourteenth century. It is entirely possible that Johann Gutenberg of Germany came across a book printed with movable type from Poland or Hungary before he adopted the idea for himself in 1458. Gutenberg became famous as the inventor of movable metal type in Europe, but the original idea came from Bi Sheng four centuries earlier.

宋

STORY
OF THE
HOUSE
OF
ZHAO

CAPITAL
CITY
KAIFENG
(NORTHERN
SONG)
HANGZHOU
(SOUTHERN
SONG)

# DIVIDED DYNASTY:
## THE SONG

NORTHERN SONG 960–1127
SOUTHERN SONG 1127–1279

**A soldier founded the Song Dynasty but scholars came to hold the power. China's enemies occupied North China. South China survived by paying tribute. Foot-binding of women began in this period.**

# THE MAN FOR THE
# YELLOW ROBE

After Tang's collapse, the leader who finally defeated all the other warlords and reunified China was a professional soldier. Zhao Kuangyin, son of a military officer, rose to become supreme commander serving the chief ruler of northern China in the city of Kaifeng. The ruler died and his seven-year-old grandson took his place.

On the morning of Chinese New Year in 960, the court received information that enemy troops were marching towards Kaifeng. Without checking whether this was true, the two prime ministers (Fan and Wang) ordered Zhao to set off with his troops to meet them. That evening Zhao and his men arrived at a desolate military outpost along the Yellow River, and set up camp. Snow was falling, it was beastly cold and there was not a single enemy soldier in sight. The troops were tired, miserable and hungry. Torn from their families without their dinner on the most important holiday of the year, they began to blame the child Emperor.

# CHINESE NEW YEAR

This is the most important holiday in China – like Christmas, New Year's Day and Thanksgiving combined. It has been celebrated for over 4000 years. In ancient times, it was the only holiday for farmers, labourers, maids and soldiers. The rest of the year they worked around the clock seven days a week.

The actual date is not fixed because China used a lunar (moon-based) calendar. It's on the first day of the first moon and falls between 21 January and 19 February. The exact date used to be announced by the Emperor himself. As the Son of Heaven, only the Emperor had the right to set the calendar. It was a major event because farmers planted their crops according to the Emperor's calendar. If the calendar was correctly set and the growing season was successful, there would be plenty of food.

Chinese families spent weeks getting ready for New Year. They would clean house, pay bills, bathe, have their hair cut and put on new clothes, usually red in colour. In the old days, many poor people could afford to eat meat only once a year. They would save their copper coins and go hungry the rest of the year for this special occasion. The main meal was eaten at a round table. If someone was absent, a place would be set for him anyway in front of an empty chair.

The holiday is celebrated in much the same way now. Special foods include rice cakes, pork, noodles, fish and dumplings stuffed with chives and pork. There is a special dessert called Eight Treasure Pudding which signifies family union. It is made with sticky rice, lotus seeds, red dates, dried candied fruits and red bean paste. In the afternoon, people visit family and friends and exchange gifts. Children are given lucky money in red envelopes.

On the streets there may be a lion dance or a dragon parade, accompanied by beating drums, cymbals, dancers, acrobats, jugglers and musicians. Firecrackers are supposed to scare away evil spirits. In the evenings, colourful lanterns dot the shopfronts and fireworks light up the sky.

Chinese New Year celebrates family and friends, and symbolises good luck and a new beginning. It is the most important holiday in China.

Next morning, the entire army gathered in front of Zhao's tent, shouting, 'We risk our lives day after day for a child who does not appreciate us! We want our commanding officer to be our Emperor! Nobody else!' When Zhao stepped out to investigate, officers draped a yellow robe over his body (yellow being a colour that only the Emperor could wear). They knelt before him and yelled over and over, 'Long live the Emperor!'

Three times Zhao refused to wear the yellow robe, but the men insisted. Zhao led his men back to Kaifeng. At the palace, the officer in charge opened the gate wide to welcome them. Face to face with the two prime ministers, Fan and Wang, Zhao burst into tears and said, 'The army forced me to do this. I feel guilty.' Fan turned away. One of Zhao's men drew his sword and exclaimed, 'The Emperor is a child. He is useless. We need a new Emperor today.' Seeing the danger, Wang dropped to his knees and Fan followed, exclaiming, 'Long live the Emperor!'

A double ceremony was held – the child Emperor abdicated and Zhao was installed as ruler in his place.

## SCHOLARS ABOVE GENERALS

Zhao granted the deposed child Emperor the title of Prince, reappointed all officials to their former posts, kept Kaifeng as his capital and formally founded the Song Dynasty with himself as First Emperor in 960 AD.

After defeating the other warlords, Zhao made his

*Distinguished Scholar in a Pasture*

best generals retire and brought their troops under his own command, thereby securing his power. He searched for talent by increasing the number of candidates and expanding the imperial examinations in a major way. Besides being given the most important policy-making jobs, the best candidates also became commanders in the army. Throughout the Song Dynasty, the ruling class consisted of scholars, not military officers. An army career was despised. Scholars were the elite of Song society.

## CANDLELIGHT SHADOWS AND AXE BLOWS

One night, the First Emperor looked out and saw a great wind blowing. He felt dizzy and anxious. When he consulted his fortune-teller, he was advised to prepare for the worst.

Alarmed, he sent for his younger brother and heir, Zhao Guangyi, at midnight. The courtiers and eunuchs could see shadows flickering in candlelight through the paper-covered windows, but couldn't hear what the two brothers were saying. Now and then, they caught glimpses of the Emperor hacking at something with an axe and his brother getting up and sitting down. From time to time, they heard a shout that sounded like 'Well done!', then a final thud which they presumed was the axe striking the ground. After that, all was silent.

Next morning, Zhao Guangyi emerged from his brother's room to announce that the Emperor had died. He took the throne as the Second Emperor of Song later that afternoon. Since that time, the phrase 'Candlelight shadows and axe blows' has become a proverb to describe unsolved mysteries.

# NO SINGING FOR THE SONG

During his 21-year reign from 976 to 997, the Second Emperor failed in two major campaigns to conquer the Liao tribe of Mongolia. He died from an arrow wound inflicted by the Liao, and left a powerful enemy at China's northern border for his son, the Third Emperor.

The Third Emperor was forced to sign a humiliating treaty with the Liao. He agreed to pay an annual tribute of nearly 3000 kilograms (100 000 ounces) of silver and 200 000 bolts of silk to the Liao. He also publicly admitted China's inferior status. The treaty resulted in a sort of peace for 100 years but all that time China paid 'hush money' to the barbarian invaders.

# RICE

In 1011, the Third Song Emperor did a revolutionary thing. He shipped 30 000 bushels of Champa rice seed, sent to him as a tribute from Vietnam, to the lower Yangzi basin. This new rice was drought-resistant and so quick-growing that farmers could get two harvests a year instead of one. Now plentiful and cheap, rice became the staple food of people living south of the Yangzi. (Northerners prefer wheat-based noodles and steamed bread, even today.) About the same time, peasants began breeding fish in their wet rice fields. Besides being tasty, fish fertilised the rice plants. Fish also ate the mosquito larvae in the rice paddies, thus lessening the risk of malaria.

# THE EMPEROR WHO LOVED TEA

In 1100 AD, the Eighth Emperor Huizong inherited the throne, after the death of his childless older brother. By then the Song had been paying tribute to the Liao for nearly a century. During the first 20 years of his reign, Huizong continued the annual payments.

Besides being Emperor, Huizong was a talented poet, painter, calligrapher and musician. He had a collection of art un-equalled anywhere in the world, including 6400 antique paintings spanning the more than nine centuries since the Han Dynasty. He was also interested in architecture,

*Listening to the Qin*

garden design and antique bronzes and jades. A great lover of tea, he wrote a booklet on the subject and made the tea ceremony popular in China. Legend has it that he discussed politics while court musicians played soothing background music. He once sent a set of 426 musical instruments to the Korean Emperor as a gift.

## SIX EVIL MEN HIDE THE TRUTH

Two subjects that Huizong did not love were foreign policy and military defence. He left that to six advisers. Nicknamed 'the six evil men', they took many bribes and became very wealthy. One of the six acquired 200 000 hectares of land bringing an annual income of 10 000 bolts of silk in just a few years. Since the Emperor believed in Daoism, they introduced alchemists who made him 'elixirs of immortality' and persuaded him to ban Buddhism throughout China. One of the worst things they did was to hide the truth from him. Despite hardship within the country and threats

*The Broken Balustrade*

of invasion from the north, they withheld any bad news. The Emperor believed his country was prosperous and peaceful, and he gave no thought to its defence. Almost every evening, they would hold lavish banquets with the most expensive food and wine. The Emperor would burn precious imported incense sticks alongside his candles, hundreds of them in a single night. Sometimes the advisers would dress up, smear makeup on their faces and sing obscene songs along with the chorus girls, court jesters and dwarf performers to make the Emperor laugh.

The people hated 'the six evil men' and made up songs to mock them.

# TREATY, THEN TROUBLE

In 1115, a new power emerged in the north, in Manchuria. They called themselves the Jin and successfully revolted against China's old enemy, the Liao of Mongolia. Emperor Huizong was delighted. He laid aside his music and paint-brushes long enough to listen to a proposal from Minister Tang, one of 'the six evil men'. China would use barbarians to conquer barbarians and form an alliance with Jin against Liao. This way, His Majesty could reassert himself and end the tribute payments at the same time. Despite warnings from many at his court, he signed the 'Treaty of the Sea' with the Jin in 1120.

The treaty said the Jin would attack the Liaos' central capital while Minister Tang would lead a force of 100 000 Chinese troops and attack the Liaos' southern capital. The result was a sound victory for the Jin but a total loss for Minister Tang.

Having witnessed the weakness of the Song army for themselves, the Jin now launched an invasion against the Song.

Emperor Huizong was terrified. He planned to flee from his capital city of Kaifeng and let his oldest son, the Crown Prince, deal with the invaders. Li Gang, one of his ministers, was shocked. He wrote a memorandum in his own blood urging Huizong to abdicate in favour of his son, who could then stay to defend the capital. Huizong reluctantly agreed. He pretended to fall and injure his right hand. Then he took a brush in his left hand and wrote, 'I am paralysed. The Crown Prince will now take the throne as the Ninth Emperor.'

# FALL OF KAIFENG, END OF NORTHERN SONG

The Ninth Emperor appointed Li Gang commander-in-chief. Under Li's leadership, Kaifeng withstood the siege. The Jin withdrew. Almost immediately, the young monarch dismissed Li Gang, thinking the Jin would be gone forever.

He was wrong. The Jin returned a few months later. In November 1126, they encircled Kaifeng for the second time. Li Gang was no longer there to organise defence. Instead, a Daoist magician appeared who claimed he could vanquish the enemy if he was given 7779 soldiers. On 25 November, the magician and his 7779 soldiers marched out of the gate. They were defeated by the powerful Jin army on the same day.

Kaifeng fell on 9 January 1127. The Jin ransacked the city and took the Ninth Emperor, his father Huizong and 3000 members of the royal court to Manchuria. They spent the rest of their lives as prisoners and never returned to China. Thus the northern Song Dynasty came to an end.

# ESTABLISHMENT OF SOUTHERN SONG

For the next 100 years, the Jin occupied Kaifeng and ruled the northern half of China. The Song Dynasty, however, did not end.

The Ninth Emperor had a younger half-brother, Prince Gou (pronounced Go), who was away from the capital when Kaifeng fell. After his father and brother were taken hostage, Prince Gou fled south and persuaded his aunt, Empress Meng, to issue an edict to enthrone him as the Tenth Emperor of Song. This aunt was the disgraced widow of the Seventh Emperor and was living outside the palace when Kaifeng fell. On 1 May 1127, Prince Gou formally re-established the dynasty (now known as Southern Song Dynasty).

To improve his public image, Emperor Gou appointed Li Gang as prime minister. Li organised army groups throughout the north, built fortresses and set up military bases. The Red Scarf Army, one of Li's guerrilla forces, made a surprise raid against the Jin and almost captured their commander-in-chief. Then the Tenth Emperor made a surprising decision. Instead of giving praise and support, he dismissed Li Gang from office.

As the ninth son of Huizong, Prince Gou had never expected to be Emperor. But fate had intervened and thrust the throne upon him. Having tasted the sweetness of power, however, he was no longer willing to step down. He was determined to hang on to his throne no matter what, even if it meant abandoning his father and brother and suffering the shame of China's defeat.

Naturally, he could not discuss this with his ministers. Publicly he proclaimed 'Death to the Jin!' But he did nothing to help those who wanted to fight them.

The Jin recognised that the Tenth Emperor was a coward. At the beginning of 1130, they marched south and sacked Nanjing and Hangzhou. The Emperor fled. He ordered a newly appointed army officer, Yue Fei, to help with the defence. To everyone's surprise, Yue Fei, only 27 years old, scored a major victory against the mighty Jin army.

After this crushing defeat, the Jin did not venture into Nanjing again. They stayed north of the Yangzi River while the Tenth Emperor made Hangzhou his capital city. Meanwhile, the Chinese people waited with bated breath for Yue Fei to defeat the Jin and reunite China.

# YUE FEI
## (PRONOUNCED EAR FEY)

### BABY IN A BARREL, THEN BULLSEYE

Soldier Yue Fei came from a poor but educated family. He was born in 1103 in a village in Henan Province, central China. A few days after his birth, the Yellow River flooded. His mother climbed into a barrel with the baby Yue Fei in her arms and floated to safety.

He was gifted in martial arts even as a child. By the age of ten, he was being trained in horseback riding, hand-to-hand combat and the use of the sword and spear. In one archery lesson the teacher shot three arrows in a row into the centre of a target. He turned to Yue Fei and said, 'If you can do this, you can call yourself an archer.' Yue Fei's arrow pierced the end of the teacher's arrow. Then he shot with his left hand and again hit the mark. The teacher was amazed. In later lessons, Yue Fei practised shooting to the left and right while galloping on a horse.

Yue Fei was determined to reclaim Kaifeng and rescue the two imprisoned emperors from the Jin. He wrote a poem titled 'Crimson Flows the River' to express his feelings of shame, anger and patriotism. It never occurred to him that the Tenth Emperor could have a different agenda.

## LONG-LEGGED QIN

Around this time, a new minister appeared at the Emperor's court in Hangzhou. His name was Qin (pronounced Chin) Kuai, his nickname 'Long-legged Qin'. Born in Nanjing, he came from a distinguished family of scholars. As a young man, he had been imprisoned by the Jin. Modern historians suspect he was recruited as their spy.

After their defeat by Yue Fei in the summer of 1130, the Jin tried a new strategy. They sent Long-legged Qin south to the court of the Tenth Emperor. His mission was to urge peace and cause conflict between the Emperor and his generals so as to weaken Song resistance.

In October 1130, Long-legged Qin suddenly appeared at the Song court with his wife. He claimed to have escaped from jail by killing a Jin guard and stealing a boat. Not long afterwards, Qin submitted a proposal titled 'How to Seek Peace with Jin' to the Emperor. The Emperor was so excited that he hardly slept. Next morning, he appointed Long-legged Qin his Prime Minister. Without a word being said on the fate of the two captive emperors, each had understood what the other really wanted.

## FOUNTAIN-HEAD OF DANGER

In 1137, Yue Fei thought the time had come for him to lead his men north, recover Kaifeng, march into Manchuria and bring back the two captured emperors. He therefore sent the Emperor a detailed plan for a major northern expedition.

Weeks went by without a reply. Yue Fei was puzzled. When the answer finally came, it was in the form of a notice informing Yue Fei that His Majesty was cancelling a promised transfer of 50 000 extra troops to Yue Fei's command.

Yue Fei was devastated. He could not understand how he had offended the Emperor. Without asking for leave, he left Nanjing abruptly to visit his mother's tomb. This was later held against him. Meanwhile, the Emperor urgently encouraged Long-legged Qin to complete peace talks with the Jin. He silenced all opposition and, under Qin's guidance, signed the humiliating Treaty of Shaoxing that year. In it, Southern Song declared itself a vassal of Jin and promised to pay tribute every year.

Among the many congratulations sent to the Emperor following the signing was a short message from Yue Fei. 'As an honest general and your loyal subject,' Yue wrote, 'I must express my deepest regrets. This peace agreement is a fountain-head of danger, not safety.'

## THE JIN CORNERED

After the signing, Long-legged Qin became the most powerful man in Southern Song. His wife was given the title Lady Wang and his son promoted to an important post. He established a secret police force to report on his enemies and suppressed all opposition with threats of violence and torture.

As Yue Fei had warned, the Jin broke the peace agreement. They launched a new offensive against Song the very next year, in 1140. The Emperor had no choice but to turn to his best general. He appointed Yue Fei chief of defence and promised to support him. Within a few weeks, Yue Fei had launched a major counter-attack and recovered a lot of territory, winning battle after battle. He pursued the Jin's best cavalry into a town only a short distance from Kaifeng. The Jin knew they were cornered. They urged their King to sue for peace and made plans to leave the city.

## VICTORY THROWN AWAY

Yue Fei and his troops set up camp near the former capital, ready for a final assault. People on both banks of the Yellow River were convinced that victory was in sight. Astonishingly, the Emperor began sending a succession of urgent messages ordering Yue Fei to withdraw. These edicts were in the form of twelve golden tablets, dispatched one after another. Yue Fei begged to be allowed to continue, arguing, 'Victory is at our fingertips. If we pull back now, the hard work of ten years will be thrown away in a single day.' But the Emperor was determined not to have his brother back on the throne. He criticised Yue Fei for being disobedient. Meanwhile, the Jin could hardly believe their luck as they watched Yue Fei's army depart.

Long-legged Qin started peace talks again. As a sign of good faith to the Jin, Long-legged Qin persuaded the Emperor to strip Yue Fei of his military rank and throw him in prison. In court, the judge charged Yue Fei and his son with treason against their country. Legend says that when he heard the judge's words, Yue Fei ripped open his jacket to reveal four characters tattooed on his back by his mother before she died. 'Serve your country with the utmost loyalty,' the court read. Even though Yue Fei remained silent, everyone present was convinced of his innocence.

*Yue Fei's tomb in Hangzhou*

# SHAMEFUL TREATY, STRANGLED HERO

The peace treaty between Jin and Southern Song was signed in November 1141. In the treaty, Song again acknowledged itself to be a vassal of Jin. It promised to pay Jin an annual tribute of 250 000 taels of silver and 250 000 bolts of silk. Kaifeng and north China remained in Jin hands. The boundary was approximately halfway between the Yellow River and the Yangzi River.

Now that the treaty was signed, the Emperor felt secure enough to kill off Yue Fei. Yet in spite of two months of torture, no evidence of treason had been discovered. Meanwhile, the Emperor was receiving daily petitions from the people calling for Yue Fei's release. Soon the judge would have to let him go.

In January 1142, Long-legged Qin and his wife were sitting at home when their maid brought in a bowl of fresh oranges. Qin's wife began to peel one and advised her husband to insert an execution order under the skin of the fruit. 'Send it to the judge tonight,' she said. 'This way, Yue Fei will be already dead before anyone can do anything.'

On 27 January 1142, Yue Fei and his son were strangled in jail. The judge reported that Yue Fei had died in captivity. When a minister demanded the reason for Yue Fei's death sentence, Long-legged Qin famously replied, '*Mo xu you*.' This phrase, meaning 'No reason needed', has become a proverb for 'trumped-up charge' in the Chinese language.

Legend has it that a street vendor was making pastries when he heard the news. He kneaded two pieces of dough into human shapes, entwined and twisted them together, then dropped them into hot bubbling oil. When passers-by asked what he was making, he said 'The husband and wife who murdered Yue Fei'. Then he took a big bite of the fried dough and laughed. These double 'doughnuts' are still made and sold in China today.

# EXPLOSION OF INVENTIONS

Southern Song never recaptured the city of Kaifeng or rescued the two emperors. The Tenth Emperor ruled for 35 years. He had no son and launched a nationwide search for descendants of the Zhao family who had not been captured by the Jin. Eventually a distant cousin, Zhao Shen, was found. In 1162, the Tenth Emperor abdicated in his favour. Seventeen years later, the Eleventh Emperor announced that Yue Fei had been a true hero and built a tomb in his memory in Hangzhou.

Hangzhou under the Southern Song Dynasty became a lively city with over a million people. (London then had a population of only 25 000.) Paintings of that time show marketplace entertainment such as acrobats, singers, puppeteers and storytellers. People also enjoyed going to social clubs, boating on the lake and visiting tea-houses.

The Southern Song government started large print shops using woodblock methods of printing. For the first time, books were cheap and readily available – so were other printed products such as playing cards, calendars, wallpaper,

graphic art and pictures of Buddhist goddesses or pagodas. Print runs of books were enormous, totalling millions of copies. Paper money, called 'flying money' because it could blow away, was also issued in huge quantities by the Song government. (Paper money was first issued in Sweden in 1661, in America in 1690, and England in 1797.)

There was an explosion of inventions, including the world's first mechanical clock, windmills, gunpowder, movable type, smallpox inoculation, odometers and textile machinery. A postal system was set up to provide swift communication. Industries such as silk, ceramics, paper goods, iron products and lacquer-ware reached high standards of perfection. The Silk Road was closed because northern China was controlled by the nomads from Manchuria and Mongolia. Nevertheless, trade by sea expanded between China, South-East Asia, India and the Arab countries. At that time, China was undoubtedly the most advanced society in the world.

With the Yangzi River as Song's first line of defence

against the Jin, the Tenth Emperor established the world's first permanent navy in 1132. Marine inventions included watertight compartments for ships, dry-dock repair, the magnetic compass for navigation at sea and pound locks for canals. Paddlewheel warships 90 metres (300 feet) long and roomy enough for hundreds of men patrolled the rivers and lakes. They were armed with mechanised catapults capable of launching enormous rocks.

Gunpowder weapons such as fire arrows, fire lances, proto-guns, grenades with pottery or bamboo casings, rockets and landmines were all developed during the Song Dynasty. In the thirteenth century, the deadly thundercrash bomb made of a cast-iron casing stuffed with gunpowder was invented. Unfortunately for Song, these weapons were captured and copied by the Mongols. The combination of gunpowder and horsemanship transformed the Mongols into a superior fighting force that almost conquered the world.

# SONG WOMEN

During the Tang Dynasty, women had opportunities (see page 81). They went horseback riding, played soccer and polo. Girls were taught to read and write, and divorce was allowed. Powerful women like Empress Wu and Consort Yang dominated court life. In the Song Dynasty, however, women's status declined. Most stayed home to bring up children and do the housework. Mothers chose husbands and wives for their children and usually lived with their oldest son until death. Girls were forbidden to sit for the imperial examination or become government ministers. They worked as inn-keepers, midwives, fortune-tellers, singers, maids and prostitutes. In the streets, they veiled their faces or rode in curtained sedan chairs.

The custom of foot-binding, which had begun in the tenth century, became widespread during Song and continued for 1000 years. Little girls' feet were bound with a long piece of cloth to keep them small. Their toes were deliberately broken and they could no longer run. Bound feet became a status symbol. Girls were told that men would not marry a woman with large, unbound feet.

Poorer women were bought and sold as maids, concubines and prostitutes. Although men could have as many wives as they could afford, women were encouraged to marry only once, even if they were widowed. For a widow, it was considered more virtuous to starve to death than to marry again.

# A FATAL WEAKNESS

Throughout the Song Dynasty, China allowed the nomads of Mongolia and Manchuria, the Jin and the Liao, to dominate them. Why?

The First Song Emperor united China after many years of warfare. To prevent his soldiers from turning into warlords, he and his heirs kept tight control over the military. Commanders were frequently rotated to keep them from bonding with their troops. Soldiers received no education and hardly any training. Recruited from the dregs of society, most of them were illiterate, poorly paid and universally despised. All major decisions were made by the scholar-ministers, not by army officers.

Throughout the Song Dynasty, there was no professional army or elite corps of officers trained in military science. Soldiers were hired mercenaries and often switched sides for higher pay.

The scholars believed that culture and civilisation were superior to military violence and would always win in the end. The Song paid tribute to the Liao and the Jin because it cost them less to pay them than to create an efficient army to fight them.

Song emperors also believed in the myth of government by virtue. Confucius had decreed that a ruler who behaved well would be successful. History proved this to be untrue. Success also required strong military leadership as well as an efficient cavalry. Southern Song had few horses and many

Song soldiers did not know how to ride. Wary of their own generals, the emperors would recall them when they proved too successful on the battlefield. As a result, the Song Empire remained culturally rich but militarily weak throughout the 300 years of its history.

In short, although Song China possessed gunpowder and manpower, it lacked the determination and will to fight. It staged spectacular firework displays yet left it to the Mongols to develop a fighting force that could employ gunpowder effectively in battle. Mongol leader Jenghiz Khan used bombs and fire-lances to destroy 90 cities of the Jin Dynasty and his son Kublai bombed his way to victory against the Southern Song.

# END OF THE SONG DYNASTY

The Song emperors made two big mistakes in foreign policy. First they allied themselves with the Jin against the Liao and became dominated by the Jin. History repeated itself 100 years later when they allied themselves with the Mongols against the Jin, using the Song's own invention, gunpowder. In 1234, the Mongols defeated the Jin, and in 1279 their leader Kublai Khan conquered all of China and established the Yuan Dynasty.

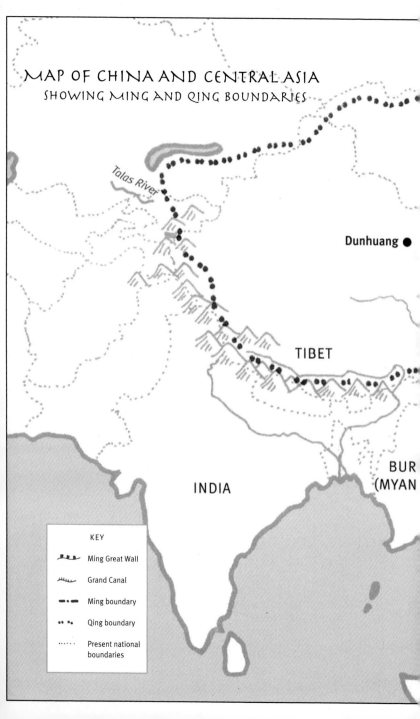

# MAP OF CHINA AND CENTRAL ASIA
## SHOWING MING AND QING BOUNDARIES

Talas River

Dunhuang ●

TIBET

INDIA

BUR
(MYAN

### KEY

| | |
|---|---|
| 🌊🌊🌊 | Ming Great Wall |
| ⌇⌇⌇ | Grand Canal |
| –·–·– | Ming boundary |
| •• •• | Qing boundary |
| ······ | Present national boundaries |

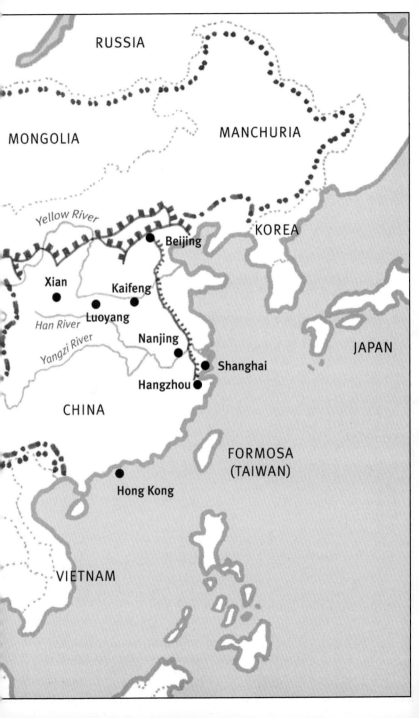

元

# STORY OF THE KHANS OF MONGOLIA

## CAPITAL CITY BEIJING

# MONGOL DYNASTY: THE YUAN

1279–1368 AD

**Mongol horsemen from the north used a Chinese invention, gunpowder, to defeat the Song. Kublai Khan built a huge, lavish palace in Beijing, but he distrusted the Chinese and tried to rule without them.**

# FROM ORPHAN TO
# UNIVERSAL RULER

Jenghiz Khan (1162–1227 AD) was born Temujin, the son of a minor Mongolian chieftain who was poisoned when Temujin was only eight years old. Left in dire poverty, his family lived on 'wild plants and mice', according to *The Secret History of the Mongols* written by an unnamed poet in the thirteenth century. Temujin was taken prisoner at the age of 13, but escaped. He grew up independent, ruthless and determined.

Mongolia at that time consisted of a large number of tribes under the rule of the Jin, a powerful tribe from Manchuria. There was no written language. A brilliant leader, Temujin united all the tribes into a single country in 1206 and adopted the Sogdian (Tibetan) script for Mongolia. At a special assembly of all the Mongol chiefs called a *kurultai*, he was elected Jenghiz Khan (Universal Ruler).

Jenghiz Khan set out to conquer the world. He organised a team of commanders loyal only to himself, each in charge of 1000 horsemen. Next he created a special corps of 10 000 bodyguards who served directly under him. This elite unit consisted of sons and brothers of his commanders.

With his army in place, he began his campaign outside Mongolia. Those who surrendered were treated as allies but those who resisted were totally destroyed. In two years, he swept across northern China and left 90 cities in ruins. In 1215 he wrecked Beijing. Legend has it that the people were massacred and the city burned for over one month.

A Mongol tale tells of Jenghiz's first siege of a walled Chinese city. He offered to leave if he were given 1000 cats and 10 000 swallows by the city dwellers. After the animals were delivered, he tied ribbons to their tails and set them alight. The terrified birds and cats fled home and set the whole city on fire. The Mongols captured the city during the ensuing confusion.

Historians doubt the truth of this tale, but it illustrates the Mongols' belief in Jenghiz's cunning.

Jenghiz Khan and his descendants dominated China, Central Asia and Eastern Europe for roughly 200 years. They recruited Russians and Central Asians to fight in China, while sending Chinese, Manchurians and Tibetans to fight in Russia. Indirectly, the conquerors brought the Muslim religion into China and introduced Chinese silk, tea and porcelain to the Middle East and the Russians.

When Jenghiz Khan died in 1227 at the age of 65, his empire stretched from the Pacific Ocean on the east to the Caspian Sea on the west. His cavalry penetrated Russia, Iraq, Iran, Turkey, Poland, Hungary and the northern half of China. Historians estimate that his armies killed 18 million people. Jenghiz's sons and grandsons continued to expand the

Mongol empire after his death.

# CASTING THEIR EYES SOUTH

A few years after Jenghiz's death, the Fourteenth Song Emperor joined forces with the Mongols and defeated the Jin (originally from Manchuria) in 1234. The last Jin Emperor fled from Kaifeng and committed suicide. Now that they were masters of northern China, the Mongols had no intention of leaving. Instead, they cast their eyes on the fertile rice fields of China's southern provinces and declared war on their former ally, Southern Song.

Kublai Khan

Two years later Kublai Khan, the 21-year-old grandson of Jenghiz Khan, was given part of Hebei Province in northern China as his personal estate. With the help of his mother, Kublai managed his territories with great skill. The two of them encouraged their Chinese subjects to farm their land, respect their elders and study Confucianism. Because of this, Kublai gained a reputation for just and benevolent rule throughout China.

For over 20 years, the Song were at peace while the Mongols were busy fighting one another and vanquishing other countries. Then Kublai Khan's older brother Mongke, who had inherited Jenghiz's title of Grand Khan, ordered him to march south and conquer Southern Song.

Kublai crossed the Yangzi River, but then received two pieces of bad news. He heard that Mongke had died suddenly, and that his younger brother Ariq was aiming to be elected Grand Khan. The Song Prime Minister, a wily character named Jia Sidao, had already been sending urgent messengers begging for a truce. Kublai decided to say yes. He granted peace to the Song in return for a yearly tribute of 200000 taels of silver and 200000 bolts of silk. Then he went back to Mongolia to fight Ariq for the title of Grand Khan.

The war between the two brothers dragged on for four years. Finally, Ariq was forced to beg for peace in 1264. Reluctant to execute his own brother, Kublai was in a dilemma as to what to do when Ariq suddenly died. Many suspected he had been poisoned.

*Kublai Khan taking part in a hunting expedition*

# KUBLAI'S PALACE

In the autumn of 1266, Kublai began the construction of his capital city in Beijing. Although the Southern Song had not yet been conquered, Kublai wanted to erect a grand palace on Chinese soil to 'command the respect of the entire Empire'.

Kublai's palace complex at Beijing (he named it Khanbalik) consisted of three gigantic squares nested one inside the other. Each was surrounded by a wall 5½ metres (18 feet) high and had eight gates. The innermost square was the Imperial Palace where Kublai lived with his family. His palace was a one-storey building with a red, yellow, blue and green roof. The walls were made of marble and covered with gold and silver. In it was an enormous central hall big enough to seat 6000 guests. (The Forbidden Palace as it exists today was built during the Ming Dynasty 140 years later at the same site.) The next square was the Tartar City for Kublai's bodyguards and soldiers from Mongolia. The outermost square of 65 square kilometres (25 square miles) was for the ordinary Chinese people.

All activity was controlled by a bell tower and a drum tower which Kublai built at the edge of his palace park in 1272. (The two towers still exist at their original sites in Beijing. The 63-tonne copper bell may be the largest bell in the world.) Starting from the Han Dynasty (and continuing for 2000 years right up to 1911), a bell had been rung at

*The drum tower (Gulou) in Beijing viewed from the bell tower (Zhonglou)*

sunrise and a drum beaten at sunset in all the major cities in China. During the Yuan Dynasty, the drum would be beaten three times at the end of the day. At the first toll, all the gates were closed. At the second toll, everyone must go inside. No one could walk on the streets except for emergencies such as childbirth or fire. At the third toll, lamps in every house in the outermost city had to be extinguished. These rules prevented the Chinese from holding secret meetings at night to plot against the Mongols.

# SIEGE BY SEESAW

In 1268, Kublai ordered the construction of an enormous river fleet of 500 boats and laid siege to the twin cities of Xiangyang and Fancheng on the Han River. These cities controlled the waterway to Southern Song's capital city of Hangzhou. The siege lasted for five years.

In 1271, while the siege was still going on, Kublai announced the beginning of the Yuan Dynasty in China with himself as the First Emperor. Although this was a serious blow to the defenders of the two twin cities, they stubbornly refused to surrender.

In 1273, Kublai suddenly remembered that one of his brothers had used a kind of seesaw catapult that flung heavy missiles to break down the walls of Baghdad and Damascus. He brought in engineers from Persia, who arrived with

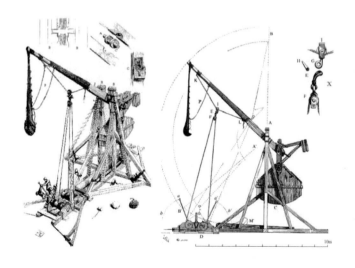

counterweight trebuchets (named *hui hui pao* or 'Muslim cannon' in Chinese) that could hurl 100-kilogram (220-pound) rocks and thundercrash bombs (gunpowder packed into metal containers) up to 500 metres (550 yards).

The Yuan army aimed their bombs at Fancheng first. The city walls crumbled as if they had been made of sand.

Yuan cavalry stormed in and killed everyone, including babies and old people. Thousands of bodies were heaped up to terrify the people watching from Xiangyang across the river.

Now the attackers turned their machine on Xiangyang. The first bomb hit a watchtower, which crashed to the ground like a toy. The Song commander, Lu Wenhuan, who had withstood five years of siege, surrendered to the Mongols in March 1273.

It was the beginning of the end for Southern Song. In 1274, Fifteenth Emperor Duzong suddenly died at the age of 34, leaving his four-year-old son as the new Emperor. Prime Minister Jia put on a show of force. He swore to defeat the Mongols and led an army of 130000 against them. He was routed in the blink of an eye, retreating to Hangzhou in humiliation and defeat. Court officials howled for his blood, blaming him for the fall of Song. He was sent into exile and died on the way there.

Empress Xie (pronounced Shie), grandmother of the child Emperor, surrendered to the Mongol General Bayan (nicknamed 'Hundred Eyes' by the Chinese) on 26 January 1276. She was taken to Beijing with her five-year-old grandson, the last Emperor of Song. Under his wife's influence, Kublai treated them kindly but he later sent the ex-Emperor away to Tibet to become a monk. Perhaps he was afraid the boy would overthrow him some time in the future. At the age of 53 the ex-Emperor committed suicide.

The ex-Emperor had two younger brothers aged four and three. They escaped south towards Vietnam with a large contingent of loyal ministers and troops. The older prince died in a storm. Three years later, the younger prince's supporters engaged the Yuan navy in a final battle at sea and lost. A Song minister strapped the imperial seal around the six-year-old prince's waist, dressed him in a gown of royal yellow, and jumped into the sea with the child on his back, off the coast of Hong Kong.

# LIFE DURING THE YUAN DYNASTY

Kublai discovered he could conquer China on horseback, but ruling the country was a different matter. Born riders and warriors, his Mongol soldiers were brave and resourceful during battles but were lost during times of peace. Many were illiterate and without the skills needed to govern a nation. They were also a tiny minority of the population. In those days, there were only 1.5 million Mongols in the entire world.

Kublai solved the problem by appointing non-Mongols to help run his armies and government, but he was wary of the Chinese. He announced that Yuan society would be divided into four racial groups. At the top were the Mongol conquerors. Next came the Central Asians (Turks, Persians, Uighurs, and Muslims from Iraq, Uzbekistan and other countries). In the third class were the Manchurians and northern Chinese (north of the Yangzi River) who had been ruled by the Jin. At the bottom were the southern Chinese, citizens of the former Southern Song

Dynasty.

Kublai carried out his business in the Mongol language and discouraged Mongols from marrying Chinese. He himself had only Mongol concubines. Reputedly, he took 30 virgins into his palace every year and ended up with 22 legitimate sons.

Mongols and Chinese people led largely separate lives. Many Mongol princes preferred to live in tents erected in the gardens of their palaces and drink fermented mare's milk instead of tea. The Chinese complained that the Mongols stank and were ill-educated, unwashed and uncouth. A large number of Chinese scholars refused to work for the Mongol government and became freelance artists, playwrights, novelists or even fortune-tellers.

Kublai was tolerant of different religions, and Buddhism and Islam both flourished under his reign. He was not so generous in other ways. The Mongols treated the Chinese very badly. Chinese people were not allowed to carry weapons. If a Chinese defended himself when attacked by a Mongol, he would be severely punished. A Mongol who murdered a Chinese could get off by paying a fine. An Italian observer, Marco Polo, wrote that the Chinese hated their Mongol rulers because they treated them like slaves.

# MARCO POLO

While Kublai was establishing his rule, two Italian traders from Venice, Niccolo and Maffeo Polo, found themselves stranded in the city of Bukhara, Central Asia. The two brothers were waiting for peace to be restored when they received a surprise invitation from Kublai Khan to visit him at his luxurious summer palace in Mongolia.

Kublai provided the

*The Polos in Bukhara*

Polo brothers with golden 'passports' which gave them safe passage while travelling on the Silk Road. Each passport was a narrow tablet 30 centimetres (1 foot) long inscribed with the Khan's orders. Those who dared to harm passport-holders would be put to death. Along the road were rest stations at which they could get fresh horses, food and water.

It took Niccolo and Maffeo one year to arrive at Shangdu, Kublai's summer palace in Mongolia. By this time, they had learnt to speak fluent Mongolese. Kublai entertained them lavishly and questioned them closely about Christianity and Western government. He asked them to deliver a letter to the Pope. In the letter Kublai expressed his interest in Christianity and asked for 100 priests to be sent to China to teach his people logic, grammar, arithmetic, astronomy, music, geometry, debate and religion.

The journey home took the brothers three years. When they finally reached Venice, they found that Niccolo's wife had died during their nine years away. His son Marco was living with relatives. In the end, only Marco was willing to accompany his father and uncle back to China to serve Kublai Khan.

In 1271 the Polos began the long trip back to China. As they journeyed, 17-year-old Marco kept a diary and recorded all he saw. The three travellers finally arrived at Kublai's summer palace in Mongolia four years later.

Kublai was delighted to meet Marco (who had learned to speak and write Mongolese, Persian, Arabic and Turkish along the way) and immediately made him one of his administrators.

Marco Polo was amazed at what he found in China. He described paper money, printing, a black stone for burning (coal), the Grand Canal, and a feast in the dining room of the Khan's palace in Beijing. The waiters wore silk masks over their

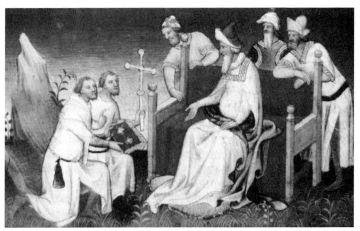

*The Polos return to China with presents from Pope Gregory X*

mouth and nose so they would not breathe or cough over the food. Silver trumpets announced Kublai's entrance and all the guests bowed low as he passed. Every time Kublai raised his wine goblet to drink, music burst forth and everyone bowed. Following the meal, the guests were entertained by acrobats, musicians and jugglers.

After serving Kublai Khan for 17 years, Marco and his uncles asked to go home to Venice. Kublai was 75 years old in 1292 and his control was waning. If his health failed, the Polos would no longer be protected.

The Polos returned by boat. They settled in Venice and Marco started work as a trader. Three years later, war was declared between Genoa and Venice. Marco joined the Venetian navy and was taken prisoner in 1298. His cellmate was a writer named Rustichello. Marco dictated his travel tales to Rustichello during the year he spent in jail in Genoa. He titled his book *A Description of the World*.

Marco became famous after his book was published. He married in his forties and had three daughters. He died at the age of 70 in Venice in 1324. Among his possessions at the time of his death was the golden passport tablet given to him by Kublai Khan for safe travel throughout the Mongol Empire.

Over the next 200 years, *A Description of the World* was translated into many languages. It was one of the first books printed by Gutenberg on his metal printing press in 1477. Maps drawn in fourteenth-century Italy depict much of Asia as described by Marco Polo. Christopher Columbus carried a copy of the book (as well as letters from the King of Spain addressed to the Grand Khan of China) when he sailed across the Atlantic Ocean in the 1490s. More importantly, Marco's book inspired Europeans to believe they could cross oceans to discover new worlds in Asia and return safely.

*Columbus wrote many notes in his copy of Polo's book*

*An Imperial Edict of the Yuan Dynasty*

# END OF THE YUAN DYNASTY

Kublai Khan was a mighty warrior and won many battles, extending his empire south-west to take over Yunnan and Tibet, but he failed to conquer Japan, Java or Vietnam. He was succeeded by his son Timur, who ruled China from 1294 to 1307. After Timur's reign, his heirs fought each other endlessly. There were many other problems. Kublai had printed his own paper money (a dollar is still called a *yuan* in China today) but too much was printed and the money became worthless. The Mongols were increasingly resented by the Chinese, especially when they favoured non-Chinese candidates in the imperial examinations which were re-established in 1315 (see pages 190–1). The Yellow River broke loose in 1314, causing severe flooding, famine and epidemics in many provinces. Hundreds of thousands of homeless peasants were forced by their Mongol masters to build sandbanks to hold the river back. These dreadful conditions led to a series of revolts. Meanwhile, bad weather caused poor harvests in the south and farmers there could not pay their taxes. Many had no choice but to leave their farms and join rebel groups. Chaos existed in China for many years until an obscure Buddhist monk named Zhu Yuanzhang seized power and established the Ming Dynasty in 1368 AD.

# MOON FESTIVAL

This festival is on the fifteenth day of the eighth month (Chinese lunar calendar) and usually falls in late September by the Western calendar. The moon is at its roundest and most brilliant, the harvest is in, and it is time to relax and celebrate. The Moon Festival has been celebrated for over 3000 years.

The fairytale behind the Moon Festival says there was once a beautiful princess named Chang O who was married to a brave archer, Hou Yi. The Emperor had given Hou Yi a pill of immortality and Hou Yi hid it. Chang O found and swallowed it and discovered she could fly. At that moment, Hou Yi returned and began to scold her. She broke away and landed on the moon. There she coughed up part of the pill which turned into a rabbit while she became transformed into a three-legged toad. Meanwhile, Hou Yi went to the sun and built himself a palace there. Every year, Hou Yi travels to the moon on the fifteenth day of the eighth moon and is reunited with Chang O for one night.

MOON FESTIVAL

Together, they rule the universe as Yin and Yang.

The Chinese believe that everything in the universe is divided according to Yin and Yang. Yin means 'shady side of a hill' and is associated with the moon and things that are female, dark and cold. Yang means 'bright side of a hill' and is linked with the sun, maleness, light and warmth. Yin and Yang are united for one night at the Moon Festival.

On the day of the Moon Festival, round fruits such as melons, oranges, peaches and pomegranates are displayed and eaten. However, the special food for this occasion is the moon cake.

A moon cake is also round. It has a crust of brown wheat flour and a filling of sweet lotus-seed paste dotted with preserved, hard-boiled duck egg yolks to represent the moon. It's sold in most Chinese food stores or restaurants during the Moon Festival.

At the time of the Yuan Dynasty, the Mongols forbade the Chinese to meet in large groups or go out at night. Legend has it that the women noticed the Mongols did not like to eat moon cakes. The people planned an uprising and wrote the date and time on pieces of paper which they inserted into the moon cakes. On the fifteenth day of the eighth month of the year 1368, the people rose up and drove out the Mongols.

This tale was not recorded in China's *Standard History* and is probably untrue, but it's a good story.

# FIREWORKS AND GUNPOWDER

The Mongols learned how to make gunpowder from the Chinese and used guns and cannons extensively in their conquests. So when and how was gunpowder invented?

Over 2000 years ago, during the Han Dynasty, people noticed that green bamboo rods thrown into a fire would erupt in loud bangs as the sticks blackened and burned. This happens because pockets of air are trapped by sap inside the hollow reeds. When heated, the air expands but cannot escape. Finally it splits the bamboo and causes a harmless explosion.

Chinese people believed that the bangs would scare away evil spirits and bring good luck. They began to burn short lengths of bamboo at Chinese New Year, weddings, birthdays and other celebrations. The Chinese name for the exploding bamboos is *bao zhu* (pronounced bough jew). *Bao* means 'exploding', *zhu* means 'bamboo'. When gunpowder was invented and firecrackers were produced, they were also called *bao zhu*.

During the late Tang Dynasty 900 years later, Daoist monks were experimenting with chemicals in their search for elixirs of immortality. They found that heating a mixture of saltpetre (named 'China snow' by Arabs but also called by its chemical name of potassium nitrate), sulphur and honey (a source of carbon) produced interesting effects. In 850, Cheng Yin wrote, 'Smoke and flames resulted. Their hands and faces were burnt. Even the whole house where they were working burned down.'

The Daoists called the mixture of saltpetre, sulphur and

*A description of the formula for gunpowder from a Song Dynasty military manuscript,* Wujing Zongyao, *written in 1044.*

carbon *huo yao* ('fire chemical'). They found that throwing a bamboo tube containing a pinch of fire chemical onto a flame produced a much louder bang than an empty tube. Later, they used paper tubes instead of bamboo and lit the firecrackers with matches. Increasing the proportion of saltpetre in the mixture made the fire chemical much more explosive and dangerous. This was how gunpowder was discovered.

火船

*Fire ships used by the Chinese navy as floating incendiaries*

During the tenth century (Song Dynasty), the Chinese began using gunpowder for military purposes. For the next 200 years, Song soldiers developed explosive bombs, fire arrows (bamboo tubes packed with arrows propelled by gunpowder), grenades, landmines and metal cannons. The oldest metal handgun in the world, dated 1288, was unearthed in China's Hei Long Jiang province.

The Mongols adopted gunpowder weapons from China and used them extensively. Coupled with their superb horsemanship, this made Mongol cavalry invincible.

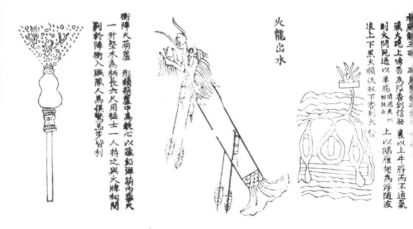

*A fire-lance ('phalanx-charging fire-gourd'), rocket ('fire-dragon issuing from the water') and naval mine ('submarine dragon king') from a 14th-century military manuscript*

Recently, a large, ancient saltpetre manufacturing base (with storage pits and fragments of china bowls and plates) was found in a network of caves in Sichuan Province. Saltpetre is abundant in the soil of those caves. It is estimated that miners could have extracted 1 kilogram of saltpetre from each 100 kilograms of soil. From there the saltpetre was probably carried to Dunhuang and then exported via the Silk Road to Mongolia, West Asia and Europe.

In the thirteenth century, a monk named William Ruysbroeck returned from China to England. He might have told his friend Roger Bacon, a fellow monk and professor at Oxford University, about the use of saltpetre in firecrackers. Eventually, Bacon was able to work out the best proportion of saltpetre, sulphur and charcoal to make gunpowder. He also realised the potential of this substance to cause death and destruction.

In Europe, advances in metallurgy, science and mathematics allowed for the rapid creation of sophisticated weapons such as muskets during the sixteenth century. From then on, the technology for the making of firearms and gunpowder in Europe surpassed that of China by leaps and bounds. By the time of the Opium War in the nineteenth century, the Chinese were so far behind that they were defenceless against a few British warships armed with guns and cannon. Awestruck and humiliated by British firepower, they had completely forgotten that it was their own ancestors who had invented gunpowder in the first place 800 years earlier.

# 明

STORY
OF THE
HOUSE
OF ZHU

CAPITAL
CITY
BEIJING

# EUNUCHS' DYNASTY: THE MING

## 1368–1644 AD

A poor Buddhist peasant-turned-warlord became the first Ming Emperor. His fourth son sent a eunuch admiral around the world in a huge treasure fleet, but later emperors abandoned trade and shipbuilding. The Great Wall was strengthened, yet it still could not keep out the nomads from the north.

# RAGS TO RICHES STORY

Zhu (pronounced Jew) Yuanzhang (1328–1398) came from a poor peasant family in Anhui Province. His was a rags-to-riches story that reads like a fairy tale. His parents  were so poor that they had to give several of their children away. When Zhu was 16 years old, the Yellow River broke through its banks, causing floods, famine and disease in Zhu's village. His parents died in the disaster and Zhu had no money to buy them coffins. He asked to join the local Buddhist monastery but the monks could not afford to keep him and sent him away. After wandering around east central China as a beggar, he returned to the monastery and lived there as a monk for three years.

In those days, the Mongols considered Buddhist temples to be hiding places for rebels. In 1352, Yuan soldiers burned Zhu's monastery to the ground. Homeless for the second time, Zhu joined the Red Turbans, a branch of the secret White Lotus Society which wanted an end to Mongol rule. He married the adopted daughter of his commander in 1354 and became the leader when his father-in-law died.

He soon captured Nanjing and used it as his base against other warlords for the next ten years. In 1368, he sent his army north and took Beijing, capital of the Yuan Dynasty.

The Mongol Emperor fled north into Mongolia with his court and was never captured. However, many Mongol nobles escaped to remote areas of China with their armies and it was not until 1382 that the last Mongol prince was driven out.

Zhu founded the Ming (meaning 'brilliant') Dynasty in the year 1368 and established his capital in Nanjing (Southern Capital). He wished to reject everything foreign and return China to the traditions of its Confucian past. After 90 years of Mongol rule, the people initially welcomed Zhu with open arms. Zhu forbade his soldiers to pillage and ordered a census of both population and land in order to assess taxes fairly. He kept down the cost of his army by giving land to his soldiers' families for farming, allowing them to be self-supporting.

Zhu was also a tyrant. He established a secret police to spy on his own officials. In 1380, he accused his chief minister of plotting against him and had the man executed. He repeatedly tried to flush out political enemies and killed over 100 000 people. Unable to trust anyone, he acted as his own prime minister and worked from dawn to dusk. In the final years of his life, he launched a final mad campaign to get rid of anyone who might challenge his successor, Crown Prince Zhu Yunwen. It was said that he executed 15 000 loyal officials and army generals before he died in 1398 at the age of 70.

Zhu's oldest son had died in 1392 and the Second Emperor was his grandson. After the Second Emperor ascended the throne, he began to reduce the size of the armies kept by his uncles. One by one, they were stripped of their military forces and put under house arrest. A year after the death of the First Emperor, Fourth Uncle Zhu Di (pronounced Judy) was the only uncle left who still had an

army. Zhu Di was a brilliant general who had proven himself in battle and won a clear victory against the Mongols in 1390. He feigned madness and refused to leave Beijing where he was stationed.

The Second Emperor sent a few army officers to Beijing to arrest two of Zhu Di's generals, accusing them of disobedience. At first Zhu Di pretended to cooperate, but as soon as he had lured the Emperor's agents into his palace, he had them executed. He then charged the Second Emperor's two chief advisers with treason, saying they had gone against the will of his dead father, the First Emperor, by persecuting him and his brothers.

Uncle and nephew went to war. Casualties were heavy. Neither side appeared able to win. After battling for two years, Zhu Di withdrew to Beijing to regroup. Around this time, help came from an entirely unexpected quarter. Zhu Di was suddenly approached by a group of unhappy eunuchs from the Second Emperor's palace in Nanjing.

# DISGRUNTLED

Before he died, the First Emperor had warned his grandson against eunuchs. He said they were mere slaves, and if given too much power, they would cause trouble. Therefore, they must never be educated or allowed to interfere with state affairs. The Second Emperor obeyed.

The Nanjing eunuchs had heard about Zhu Di. They wanted to know whether it was true that the Prince's most trusted adviser was a eunuch named Ma Sanbao? Was it also true that Zhu Di was setting up a special school to educate eunuchs? How lucky!

They themselves were tired of being beaten and abused day after day. The Second Emperor treated them like dirt and refused to educate them. So they had fled north to Beijing to give Zhu Di the information he needed to win the war.

Under their guidance, Zhu Di launched a bold new campaign in January 1402 with the eunuch Ma Sanbao as one of his chief military strategists. He avoided all those cities that the eunuchs said were heavily fortified and took the easy road south along the Grand Canal. Soon he and his army had crossed the Yangzi River and surrounded Nanjing. Shortly after his arrival, the eunuchs persuaded two of the Second Emperor's generals to defect to Zhu Di's camp and discuss a secret peace. With their help, Zhu Di entered the city peacefully on 13 July 1402.

As he approached the Imperial Palace in Nanjing, he saw the building in flames. Inside, he found the charred bodies of the dead Empress and her oldest son. There was a third body but it was so badly burnt it was unrecognisable. There were rumours that the Second Emperor had escaped as a Buddhist monk and fled overseas.

Zhu Di ascended the throne on 17 July 1402 and announced that the years of rule by his nephew had simply not existed. The reign of his father, the First Emperor, had ended not in 1398, but in 1402. Those who disagreed or questioned Zhu Di were punished with 'death to the ninth degree' (death to the culprit, his spouse, his parents, uncles and aunts, parents-in-law, his siblings, their spouses, his children, their spouses).

After he became Emperor, Zhu Di rewarded all the eunuchs who had helped him. He remembered that Ma Sanbao had been especially valiant during the siege of Beijing in 1399. Zhu Di's horse had been killed at a place called Zheng Lun Ba, immediately outside Beijing, and Ma had come to his rescue. As Emperor, Zhu Di granted his servant the special surname of Zheng (pronounced Jung) to commemorate the incident. He also made him head of the palace eunuchs. From then on, Ma San-bao was called Zheng He, a name which was to become famous.

*A Ming Dynasty emperor watching the court eunuchs playing* cuju *football*

# ADMIRAL ZHENG HE
## (PRONOUNCED JUNG HUH)

Admiral Zheng He (or Ma Sanbao) was the descendant of a Turkic Muslim from Uzbekistan named Sayyid Ajall al-Din Omar. Sayyid's grandfather had surrendered to Jenghiz Khan with 1000 horsemen when Sayyid was nine years old. Sayyid served in the Mongol army during its invasion of north China and learned to speak fluent Mongol and Chinese.

Thirty-three years later, in 1253, Kublai Khan conquered the Kingdom of Dali (now Yunnan Province). Yunnan is bordered by the Azure Mountains on one side and the Erhai (ear-shaped lake) on the other. Famous for its stony mountains and clean water, Yunan is home to 24 different tribes. The marble quarried there is so beautiful and plentiful that the name for marble in Chinese is *Dali shi* (stones from Dali).

In 1273, Kublai appointed Sayyid as Governor of Yunnan. Sayyid built many Confucian temples and Muslim mosques throughout Yunnan during his governorship. He and his children also introduced Islam into that area. They constructed a road across the mountains to Arabia so Muslims could visit Mecca. Today over half a million Muslims live in Yunnan. Many Chinese Muslims also settled in neighbouring Burma (Myanmar).

Sayyid's fifth son, Masuh, changed his name to Ma. For five generations, the Ma family continued to work on behalf of the Mongols as tax-collectors and administrators in Yunnan.

Ma Sanbao's father and grandfather both married Chinese women. The two men were devout Muslims and had made pilgrimages to Mecca. The Ma family spoke both Persian and Chinese at home.

Ma Sanbao was taken prisoner at the age of 11 during a war between the Ming army's General Fou and a Mongol prince who had fled to Yunnan. Impressed by the child's courage and quick wit, Fou had Ma Sanbao castrated. He then gave the boy to Prince Zhu Di as his servant. (It was the custom during the Ming Dynasty to castrate the enemy's young sons if they were taken prisoner. Castration was a brutal affair carried out with a curved knife that cut off the penis as well as both testes in one stroke. Afterwards, the boy would be incapable of having children. Infection of the wound often followed and many boys died from the procedure. Those who survived became eunuchs and were employed as palace servants.)

From then on, Zhu Di and Ma Sanbao spent much time together in army tents around the country. They developed a close friendship while battling first the Mongols, then the army of the Second Emperor.

In 1403, the year after he became Emperor, Zhu Di ordered shipyards in several cities to build and refit a fleet of over 1600 ships (nicknamed 'the Treasure Fleet') for ocean explorations. A frenzy of shipbuilding ensued for the next five years. At one time, 30 000 skilled craftsmen lived and worked at the Nanjing shipyard. The best shipwrights, carpenters, sailmakers, iron-smiths and caulkers were transferred there from all over the country. Within the shipyard were seven huge dry docks, separated from the Yangzi River by high dams. When a ship was completed, a gate in the dam would be opened to flood the dock and allow the ship to move easily into the Yangzi. The largest ships were longer than a football field (six times as long as the ships sailed by Columbus 90 years later) and carried nine masts. A Chinese historian described them as being 'as big as houses'. With their sails unfurled, he wrote, 'the fleet blocked the sun and looked like giant clouds in the sky'.

The first voyage was launched in 1405. The new Emperor appointed his favourite eunuch, Ma Sanbao, now Admiral Zheng He, supreme commander of an entire fleet of 317 ships and crew of 26 800 men. Sixty-two of the ships were treasure ships with staterooms. Each weighed 3000 tonnes, had up to 50 cabins and was 137 metres (440 feet ) long (longer than a standard football field). There were also warships, troop carriers, patrol boats, horse transporters, supply ships and water tankers. The Emperor gave Zheng He the title of 'Admiral of the Western Seas'. The ships were to go far and wide and demonstrate the wealth and might of the Ming Empire to the entire world.

Although strongly armed, Admiral Zheng's ships did not set out to conquer or colonise the countries he visited. He was more like a goodwill ambassador than a naval warrior. Some historians believe Zhu Di wanted the fleet to search for his missing nephew (in case he hadn't been burned in the palace fire). Between 1405 and 1433, Zheng made seven voyages. He never found the Second Emperor.

By all accounts, Admiral Zheng was a big and handsome man over 2 metres tall (6 feet 6 inches), with a booming voice and a belly measuring 1.5 metres around. Under him were eunuch ambassadors and eunuch assistant directors. The army commander reported to a eunuch supervisor. It was the first time in Chinese history that a eunuch had been placed in such an important position. Zhu Di never forgot the eunuchs' vital role in his war against the Second Emperor.

Zhu Di trusted Admiral Zheng so much that he gave him several blank scrolls stamped with his seal of office. The orders Admiral Zheng wrote on these scrolls would automatically carry the authority of the Emperor.

Zheng He's orders were to

- display the might of the Ming Emperor to 'All Under Heaven'
- make every country pay tribute to China
- calculate distances and routes between China and other lands, and add to geographic knowledge
- spread Chinese culture abroad
- establish law and order on the high seas.

The boats carried soldiers, sailors, doctors, pharmacists, shipwrights, scribes and translators. The sailors grew their own vegetables in plant boxes on board. There is evidence that Admiral Zheng's men did trade goods with other

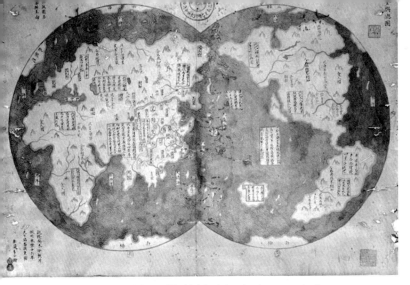

*A Chinese map of the world which is claimed to be a reproduction
of a 15th century map of Admiral Zheng He's travels*

countries. In one journey, Zheng brought back a giraffe from Africa which lived for many years in the palace grounds.

Communication at sea between ships was by sight and sound. Every ship had its own flag as well as signal bells, banners, drums, gongs, lanterns and carrier pigeons. Drums would warn the entire fleet in case of a storm. Lanterns signalled one another in the dark or in bad weather. Carrier pigeons communicated with folks back home. Navigation at sea was carried out by a water compass: a magnetised needle floating in a basin of water. Time was measured by burning graded incense sticks. They found their latitude by calculating the angle between the position of certain well-known stars and the horizon; and gauged their distance from shore by using a sounding line to determine the depth, smell and nature of the sand below.

Admiral Zheng visited Singapore, Vietnam, Malacca, Java, Sri Lanka, India, the Persian Gulf and the east coast of Africa. Although a Muslim, he respected all religions. He left stone tablets in some countries inscribed with Chinese characters to commemorate his visits. The one he brought to Sri Lanka was inscribed in three languages, each respectfully addressing a separate religion:

- ❋ a Chinese paragraph to the Lord Buddha
- ❋ a Tamil paragraph to the Hindu god Siva
- ❋ a Persian paragraph to Allah and the saints of Islam.

## RISE OF THE EUNUCHS

Besides exploring distant countries across the ocean, the Third Emperor also moved his capital city from Nanjing to Beijing. This was a massive undertaking involving over

one million labourers. Beijing's Purple Forbidden Palace, constructed on the same site as Kublai Khan's palace, was formally opened on Chinese New Year's Day 1421. (This is the palace you will visit if you go to Beijing.)

The new palace did not bring happiness to the Third Emperor. Soon after he moved into his new home, lightning struck three great halls and burned down 250 rooms. News also reached him that the enormous expenses of the Treasure Fleet, the Forbidden Palace and fighting in Vietnam and Mongolia were bankrupting the country and causing hardship among his people. There were reports of famine as well as an epidemic which caused 250 000 deaths.

Despite all these disasters and his own poor health, the Third Emperor embarked on three new campaigns against rebellious Mongols at China's north-western border during the last three years of his life. Finally in August 1424, he died in inner Mongolia. His body was carried back to Beijing in a makeshift tin coffin. There it was transferred

*The Forbidden City in Beijing*

to a wooden casket and buried in the Ming tombs a little way out of Beijing. Sixteen of his concubines were forced to commit suicide and were buried with him.

Admiral Zheng was away at sea when the Third Emperor died. On his return to China, he found Zhu Di's 46-year-old eldest son on the throne. The Fourth Emperor was by nature frugal and conservative. He cancelled all future voyages planned for the treasure ships and sent the sailors home.

Barely nine months later, the Fourth Emperor became ill and died suddenly (probably of a heart attack). On his deathbed, he said, 'I can't bear to burden my people with more taxes. My tomb must be constructed with the greatest simplicity.' His son became the Fifth Emperor.

Against the advice of his scholar-officials, the Fifth Emperor sent Admiral Zheng on his seventh and last voyage in 1432. Zheng died the next year and was buried at sea before the treasure fleet returned. The legend of Sinbad the Sailor from *One Thousand and One Arabian Nights* may have been based on Zheng's life. Zheng's birth name was Ma Sanbao (Sinbad). He and Sinbad were both Muslim sailors who made seven voyages to distant lands.

By then, the scholar-officials and the eunuchs loathed one another. A special school had been set up to educate the eunuchs in subjects such as the management of imperial workshops and the printing of official documents. Soon the eunuchs had their own civil service parallel to the government's but not controlled by it. The head eunuch became a sort of chief of staff who made out the Emperor's schedule. He and his fellow eunuchs influenced the Emperor on many key decisions. Some eunuchs became so powerful that they would challenge the Emperor's cabinet. This led to bitter quarrels between the two groups.

The Fifth Emperor died in 1435 after reigning for ten years, leaving the throne to his seven-year-old son. The Sixth Emperor came under the complete control of his tutor, the eunuch Wang Zhen, who used his position as head eunuch to become guardian of the child Emperor and dictator of China.

In 1449, Wang Zhen led the 22-year-old Sixth Emperor and half a million troops into enemy territory to teach the Mongols a lesson. On the way, they were ambushed by Mongol horsemen. The Mongols killed Wang Zhen and took the Sixth Emperor prisoner.

Back in Beijing, the Minister of War hurriedly organised a successful Chinese resistance against the Mongols and established the Sixth Emperor's younger brother as the Seventh Emperor. During the first audience at the new Emperor's court, a violent quarrel broke out between pro-Wang-Zhen eunuchs and anti-Wang-Zhen officials. A large group of enraged officials pounced on three powerful eunuchs and killed them with their bare hands in front of the shocked and fearful young monarch.

A year later, the Sixth Emperor was returned to Beijing unharmed by the Mongols. Six years after that, he staged a coup, deposed his brother and re-ascended the throne. He executed the minister of war who had installed his brother as Emperor, and built a shrine in memory of his dead tutor Wang Zhen.

Meanwhile, political struggles continued between eunuchs and scholars at court. Ships and overseas trading were traditionally controlled by the eunuchs. By cutting down on these activities, the officials thought they were scoring major victories against their rivals. There were no more voyages after 1433. No money was allocated for shipbuilding or new technology. Shipyards became derelict and were shut down. The number of ships dwindled. There is evidence that Admiral Zheng He's travel records were deliberately destroyed by the vice-president of the war ministry 40 years after his death.

Half a century later, it became an offence punishable by death to build ships with more than two masts or to leave the country. There was a surge of lawlessness all along the coast. With no navy patrolling the waters, gangsters ruled the waves.

The Chinese Navy under Admiral Zheng had the potential to become the greatest seafaring power in the world. Instead, China deliberately stepped back just as the great age of navigation dawned around the globe.

In 1492, Christopher Columbus sailed for China in three small boats totalling 450 tons. Taking a western route, he discovered America instead. In 1519, the Portuguese Ferdinand Magellan sailed around South America and reached the Pacific Ocean. But while Europe was making exciting new discoveries with these voyages of exploration and its scientific revolution, China turned inward.

# TRADE BAN IGNORED

The Southern Song and the Yuan had encouraged coastal shipping and trade in every way they could. After the death of Admiral Zheng He, the officials of the Ming court took a totally different approach. They tried to keep out all foreigners. In 1449 and 1452, the Ming Emperor proclaimed that any merchant attempting to engage in trade with foreigners was a pirate and would be executed if caught. China closed its doors to the world.

It was no use. Japanese, Portuguese, Spanish, Dutch, English and Chinese merchants ignored the ban and traded with one another all along the coast. China imported Mexican silver, Indian spices, New World plants and European instruments such as clocks and glass prisms, while exporting tea, silk and porcelain.

# PORCELAIN

During the Ming Dynasty, many Europeans and Japanese were first introduced to porcelain plates, cups and bowls. They loved eating and drinking from them so much that they named the dishes after the country which first invented and produced them: China or China ware.

What is porcelain? If you mix clay with water and bake it in an oven you get pottery, but not all pottery is porcelain. Porcelain is shiny, beautiful and impervious to water, resembling glass. It has been made in China since the second century AD.

Since ancient times, a city called Jingdezhen has been known as the 'porcelain capital of China'. The city was named after the Third Emperor of the Song Dynasty. In 1004, he had a special kiln built there which continued to produce porcelain for China's emperors until the fall of the Qing Dynasty 900 years later. This delicate and beautiful china was much prized for export. It was said to be 'white as jade, bright as a mirror, and thin as paper'.

In 1712 a French Jesuit priest D'Entrecolles reported that Jingdezhen was heavily polluted, with 'volumes of smoke and flame ... Approaching at night, the scene reminds one of a burning city in flames, or of a huge furnace.'

Methods of porcelain manufacture were a closely guarded trade secret, but he revealed that two substances found nearby were crucial: china clay (kaolin) and china stone. The china stone had to be ground to a powder and mixed with the clay in the correct proportions before being fired at very high temperatures. The fusion of the two gave Chinese porcelain its unique lustre and translucency. Ceramics made from kaolin without china stone or vice versa was like 'having a body without bones to support its flesh', according to a Chinese merchant.

You can identify porcelain from the various dynasties relatively easily. Tang Dynasty ware is famous for its three-coloured (green, yellow and amber) figures of grooms, camels, horses and warriors. Song Dynasty produced black tea ware, clear white bowls and exquisite celadon (pale green) dishes. In the fourteenth century, Arab merchants brought cobalt blue pigment from Persia to China, and this made possible the famous blue-and-white patterns of late Yuan and Ming Dynasty porcelain. During the Qing Dynasty, new technology allowed multicoloured enamel paintings of dragons, birds and flowers to be superimposed on the surface of porcelain.

In Europe, porcelain was first produced during the eighteenth century in direct imitation of the Chinese process. Made in Germany, it was known as Dresden or Meissen china.

# KOWTOWING BEFORE AN EMPTY THRONE

Because Ming authorities were unable to patrol all of China's long coastline, any merchant with a boat could smuggle goods into the country. Piracy became rampant. Japanese and Chinese pirates raided the coastal cities at will during the first half of the sixteenth century. Piracy diminished only after China lifted its ban on sea trade and started establishing official trading posts.

*From a European book,* China monumentis illustrata *(1667); Matteo Ricci is on the right*

One of these trading posts was set up by the Portuguese in Macau in 1577. The brilliant Italian priest Matteo Ricci arrived there a few years later. He learned to read and write Chinese in an incredibly short time. Within a few years, he had composed a Chinese–Latin dictionary, translated the Confucian classics into Latin, and inscribed a series of books in Chinese. He also drew a map of the world with China at the centre. Ricci was finally accepted by the Ming court and granted an audience with the Emperor early one morning in 1602.

Matteo Ricci, dressed in elaborate

robes suitable for the occasion, solemnly kowtowed at dawn before an empty throne. (The kowtow was an act of respect shown to the Emperor by kneeling and touching one's forehead to the ground.) The Emperor Wanli, who had ruled China since he was a nine-year-old, had become bored with his job after 30 years. He hid from the world like a spoilt child and left the day-to-day administration of his country to his eunuchs. They gained extraordinary power because they were the only contact between the Emperor and the outside world.

Despite his refusal to meet face to face with Ricci, the Emperor was delighted with Ricci's gifts, including a clock that chimed. He granted Ricci access into the Forbidden Palace (the only Westerner so favoured up to that time) to teach the eunuchs about the maintenance of the clock and to play the clavichord. He also gave Ricci a monthly wage and a burial site in Beijing.

Emperor Wanli (1563–1620), the Thirteenth Ming Emperor, governed wisely for the first ten years under the guidance of Minister Zhang Juzheng. He extended the Great Wall to its greatest length and spent so much money on its repair and maintenance that the name for the Great Wall in China became Wanli Chang Cheng. (Pronounced

*Emperor Wanli enjoying a boat ride with guards and courtiers*

in Chinese, this could mean the Great Wall of Wanli or the Great Wall of Ten Thousand *Li* – a *li* is a measurement of length, about 500 metres, or 550 yards.)

Minister Zhang died when Wanli was 19. For the next 18 years he attended to his duties and ruled the country to the best of his ability. But then he lost all interest in state affairs, as Ricci found out. He became wildly selfish and extravagant, diverting public funds for his personal use. He spent nine million ounces of silver on building his royal palaces but failed to pay his army and government officials. In 1619, the Ming army lost a crucial battle against the Manchus. The Manchus were clamouring at the gate of the Great Wall but Wanli did not seem to care. He had grown very fat and there were rumours that he was addicted to opium. He died in 1620 and was buried in the Ming tomb with two of his wives.

# WAR ON TWO FRONTS

Emperor Tianqi ascended the throne after the death of Wanli. Aged 15, he was much influenced by the notorious eunuch Wei Zhongxian and Wei's friend Madame Ke, the Emperor's wet-nurse. Tianqi was only interested in carpentry and willingly transferred his authority to Wei. As Grand Secretary of State, Wei unleashed a reign of terror for several years. He took bribes, levied taxes and persecuted anyone who dared to oppose him. Wei's rule ended in 1627 when Tianqi died. Banished by the next Ming Emperor, Chongzhen, Wei committed suicide.

When Chongzhen, the seventeenth and last Ming Emperor, ascended the throne in 1627, he found himself in deep trouble. His treasury was almost empty after all the military campaigns in Mongolia, Korea and Vietnam. Bad weather and poor harvests led to widespread famine and disease in many provinces. Inside his court, the eunuchs and scholar-officials were battling one another at every turn. The cost of maintaining his royal relatives (over 23 000 clansmen on annual pensions) was astronomical. On his northern border, he was being harassed by Mongol as well as Manchurian nomads. Meanwhile, unpaid soldiers and army deserters terrorised villagers throughout the country.

By the 1640s, troops of the Ming Empire were fighting a war on two fronts: against Manchu cavalry in the north-east and peasant rebels in the north-west.

# END OF THE MING DYNASTY

In the end, the Ming Dynasty fell because of a beautiful woman. Her name was Chen Yuanyuan, and she was a concubine to General Wu Sangui, the last loyal Ming commander defending the Great Wall against the Manchus.

General Wu San-gui was stationed at Shan Hai Guan (Gateway of Mountain and Sea), the main north-eastern passageway between China and Manchuria in the Great Wall. Wu came from a family of career soldiers. By 1644, he was the only general still faithful to the Ming court. All the rest, including his own uncles and cousins, had surrendered to the Manchus.

On 22 April 1644, the Emperor heard that Jurong Pass, a mere 65 kilometres (40 miles) north of the Forbidden Palace, had been taken by the Chinese warlord Li Zi-cheng whose army was fast approaching Beijing. Panic-stricken, the Emperor sent word to General Wu to return to the capital immediately with his troops.

Two days later, the Emperor received a message from Warlord Li. In return for one million ounces of silver and the right to rule as King in north-west China, Li was prepared to fight the Manchus on behalf of the Emperor.

The Emperor refused this offer. Instead, he announced the end of the Ming Dynasty and advised his ministers to commit suicide. He returned to his rooms and spent the day drinking. His Empress hanged herself but his daughter Princess Chang Ping refused to die by her own hand. Enraged, the Emperor swung his sword and cut off her left arm.

At dawn, he appeared for his usual morning audience dressed in his imperial robes, but none of his ministers came. He left the palace through a back gate with a loyal eunuch, climbed a mound called Coal Hill in nearby Jingshan Park, entered the red pavilion at the top of the hill and prepared to hang himself from a tree with his sash. Before he died he said to the eunuch, 'I invite the bandits to cut up my body but I forbid them to harm any of my subjects. I will not be emperor of a conquered nation but my subjects will have to resign themselves to such a fate. I have treated all of my ministers well and yet, on this day, not a single one is here with me.' After his death, a note was discovered on his body. It contained two characters scrawled in his own hand: *TIAN ZI* (Son of Heaven).

# THE BEAUTIFUL CONCUBINE AND THE GENERAL – A TRAGIC LOVE STORY

Meanwhile, a jubilant Li Zi-cheng entered Beijing with his unruly followers. After discovering the Emperor's body, he asked for General Wu. Hearing that Wu was still at his post at the Great Wall, he immediately went to Wu's Beijing residence. There he seized Wu's father and his beloved concubine, the beautiful Chen Yuanyuan.

Warlord Li proceeded to send General Wu two letters.

The first was from a surrendered former Ming general praising Li's character. The second was from General Wu's father urging him to join Li's army. Accompanying the letters were 10 000 ounces of silver and 1000 ounces of gold.

Legend has it that Wu was on his way to join Warlord Li in Beijing when he heard that Li had seized Chen Yuanyuan for his own harem. Mad with jealousy, General Wu turned back and appealed to the Manchus for help. One week later, Wu opened the gates and admitted the Manchu forces. Together, their combined armies fought a huge battle against Li and defeated him on 27 May 1644.

*Ming court ladies*

Li retreated back to Beijing. There he crowned himself Emperor on 4 June, beheaded Wu's father, set fire to the Forbidden Palace and rode away with Chen Yuanyuan.

Next morning, the Manchu army entered the Forbidden Palace, ceremoniously buried the last Ming Emperor in the Ming tombs and proclaimed the dawn of a new dynasty: the Qing (pronounced Ching) Dynasty.

Chen Yuanyuan escaped and later went into a nunnery, blaming herself for the fall of the Ming Dynasty. Warlord Li was relentlessly pursued by General Wu's forces and died in 1645. The Manchus rewarded Wu with the title of King of Yunnan Province. He served them for 30 years but eventually rebelled and declared himself Emperor. He died of natural causes in 1678.

# THE GREAT WALL

In 221 BC, the First Emperor of China defeated all the other states and united China. That night he dreamed he was flying on a magic carpet towards the moon. Below him was his kingdom, bordered by tall mountains to the west, the Yangzi River to the south and the ocean to the East. But what about the north? There was no barrier between the arid grasslands inhabited by the Xiong Nu (fierce tribesmen of Mongolia, also called Huns) and the fertile farmlands of Qin's hard-working peasants.

When he woke, the Emperor summoned his most capable general, Meng Tian, and ordered him to build the Great Wall of China.

Meng Tian was put in charge of 300000 soldiers and 500000 civilians. In seven years, he built a wall which followed the ups and downs of the land for 2500 kilometres (1500 miles).

It was an enormous undertaking. Chronic hunger, cold and tiredness added to the workers' misery. Many died and were buried in trenches nearby. The Great Wall became known as the 'longest cemetery on earth'.

Later dynasties built sections of wall at different places. Some of those may have been incorporated into the final Great Wall, but long stretches collapsed and disappeared over the centuries. The continuous structure we see today is less than 600 years old. Most of it was built during the Ming Dynasty (1368–1644) to keep out the Mongol people to the north.

The First Ming Emperor began a massive campaign to rebuild the Great Wall. Nine of his sons were sent to serve as commanders at the frontier. After his death, his son (the Third Ming Emperor) took the throne from his nephew and moved the capital from Nanjing to Beijing, only 20 kilometres (12 miles) from the Great Wall.

For the next 250 years, a succession of Ming emperors built and repaired the Great Wall. Brick or stone covered its sides and on top, providing a paved walkway 6 metres (20 feet) wide and 8 metres (26 feet) above ground. Local materials such as stone blocks, bricks, wooden planks, tiles and dirt were used. Watchtowers, battlements, flights of stairs and garrison buildings with drains were part of the structure. The wall swooped from steep mountain passes to gentle valleys, from green grasslands to dry deserts, beside rushing rivers and marshy swamps.

In 1644 General Wu, the last Ming commander, opened the gates of Shan Hai Guan (Gateway of Mountain and Sea) and welcomed the Manchu army into China. When it really mattered, the Great Wall failed because of human frailty.

The Manchus' defeat of China meant the end of the Great Wall as a defensive barrier against her northern neighbours. Nomads were now the masters of China as well as Manchuria and Mongolia.

During the nineteenth century, traders, missionaries and diplomats from Europe and America visited China in increasing numbers. Westerners were enthralled by China's rich history and culture. Gradually, the Great Wall emerged as a symbol of the might and glory of China's past.

In 1899, four reporters were waiting at a railroad station in Denver, Colorado to meet a visitor. When the visitor failed to arrive, the reporters decided to invent a story. They wrote of a group of American engineers who were passing through Denver on their way to China. Why? The Emperor of China had invited them. For what purpose? They were going to tear down the Great Wall as a gesture of goodwill from the Chinese Emperor to encourage trade with Westerners.

Next morning, the headlines read 'Great Chinese Wall Doomed'. The false story travelled from Denver to New York to Beijing. Peasants in China became outraged. A secret Chinese society known as the Boxers erupted in a bloody uprising against foreigners in 1900. An army of 18 000 troops from eight nations were sent to Beijing to crush the rebels. This story demonstrates the vital role played by the Great Wall in the hearts and minds of the Chinese.

In 1911, the Qing government was toppled by Sun Yat-sen, who founded the Republic of China. He and his successors adopted the Great Wall as China's national symbol, saying that it had preserved China's civilisation for over 2000 years.

During his struggles against Chiang Kai-shek, the Communist leader Mao Zedong adopted a song which glorified the Great Wall as a symbol of China's national spirit. In 1966, however, Mao unleashed the Cultural Revolution to subdue his rivals. During a period of almost ten years, books were burnt, antiques were smashed and hundreds of kilometres of Great Wall were demolished. After Mao's death in 1976, Deng Xiaoping took power. In 1984, Deng publicly announced, 'Let us love our country and restore our Great Wall.'

People used to believe that the Great Wall was visible from outer space. Astronauts say this is not true. Today it lives in our minds as a symbol of the Chinese will to endure.

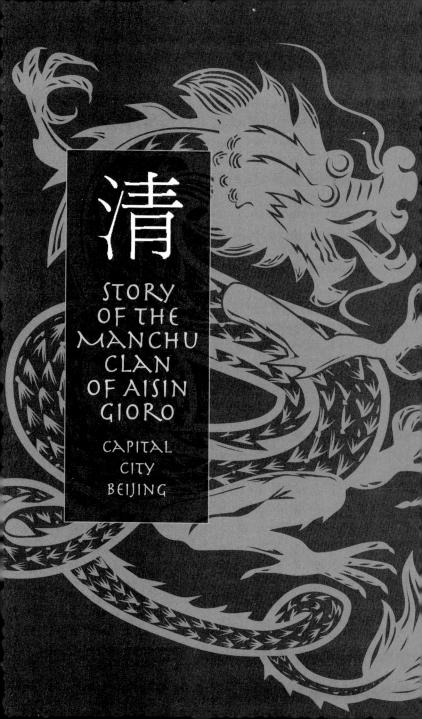

清

# STORY OF THE MANCHU CLAN OF AISIN GIORO

## CAPITAL CITY BEIJING

# CRIPPLED DYNASTY: THE QING

Manchu people from north of the Great
Wall founded a new dynasty, the Qing,
and decreed that every Chinese man must
wear a pigtail. They ignored the outside
world, stuck to the old ways and paid for
their pride in a humiliating defeat. The last
Qing Emperor abdicated in 1912, aged six.

The Manchus were also known as the Jin. They descended from the same tribe that had kidnapped Emperor Huizong and his son in 1127. By the 1600s, they were again threatening China. As we saw in the previous chapter, the last loyal Ming general, General Wu, opened the gate of the Great Wall for the Manchu army to march in and take over.

## THE PIGTAIL TEST

The Manchu ruler was six-year-old Shunzhi (pronounced Shun-jer). In October 1644, Shunzhi was proclaimed First

Emperor of the Qing Dynasty, in Beijing. A year later the new government decreed that every Chinese male in the land had to shave his forehead and wear a queue (pigtail). Those who did not do so within ten days would be beheaded. In this way, the conquerors could tell at a glance who had given in and who had not; who was loyal to Qing and who was not. From then until the end of the Qing Dynasty in 1911, every Chinese man wore a pigtail. Marriages between Manchu and Chinese people were not allowed.

In other ways, life went on much as it had under the Ming.

The new Emperor's advisers re-established the examination system, appointing the best candidates as magistrates no matter what group they came from. When he grew up, Emperor Shunzhi employed Han Chinese as tutors to his children. Manchu emperors learned the Chinese classics, and gradually forgot their own language. Shunzhi's descendants all admired Chinese culture and tried to preserve it by resisting change of any kind.

In spite of this, the majority of Han Chinese people saw the Manchus as barbarian foreigners and resented their rule. Resistance was strongest in the south. As a result, the Qing Dynasty regarded all southerners as rebels, especially those living along the coast.

In 1661, Shunzhi died of small-pox, aged 24. His son Kangxi (xi is pronounced she), regarded as a model emperor, ruled for 61 years. He took over Taiwan and Tibet and suppressed the Mongols. Under Kangxi and his son and grandson, China enjoyed 150 years of peace. However, the population had doubled to 400 million by 1850. There was not enough food. The peasants were driven to desperation by hunger and disease.

# 'WE POSSESS EVERYTHING, AND HAVE NO USE FOR YOUR COUNTRY'S GOODS'

The Qing turned their backs to the outside world. They forbade all travel outside China. Anyone who left could be executed when they returned. The Qing also continued the Ming ban on sea trade. Commerce with foreigners was restricted to one port, Guangzhou, in the months from October to January. No foreign ships were allowed to sail up the Pearl River. Chinese people were forbidden to teach foreigners the Chinese language and not allowed to socialise with them.

*Emperor Kangxi seated on deck on a sea tour*

Meanwhile, trade between China and the rest of the world was expanding at an amazing rate. In the early 1700s, 180 tonnes (400 000 pounds) of tea was sold every year. Seventy-five years later, this had grown to 10 600 tonnes (23 400 000) pounds. Huge amounts of silver flowed into China in exchange – 450 000 kilograms or 16 million ounces in the 1780s.

# SPILT TEA AND INDEPENDENCE

For much of the eighteenth century, America was a colony of Great Britain. Americans were not allowed (by Britain) to buy tea directly from China but had to go through the British East India Trading Company in London. American merchants bitterly resented the enormous amounts of tax they had to pay Britain for Chinese tea. In 1773 they protested by dumping shiploads of tea into Boston Harbor. This incident, known as the Boston Tea Party, eventually led to the War of Independence and birth of the United States of America.

In 1793, King George III of England sent Lord Macartney to visit Emperor Qianlong (pronounced Chien) in order to improve trade relations between China and Great Britain. Lord Macartney took with him 84 servants and 600 cases of gifts. It must have been a grand occasion, because Macartney wrote in his diary, 'I have seen King Solomon in all his glory.' Macartney refused to kowtow but presented King George's letter to the Emperor in a gold box studded with diamonds. He waited patiently in his lodgings for three weeks. Finally, the answer arrived. It was delivered by palace eunuchs dressed in their finest robes carrying a chair covered in yellow silk. Sitting on the chair was not a person, but the Emperor's letter in reply. The Emperor had politely turned down all of Macartney's requests for increased trade and contact between Britain and China. 'We possess everything,' the Emperor announced grandly, 'and have no use for your country's goods.'

Macartney sailed away without achieving any of his goals. However, on his return journey downriver, he was

The Qianlong Emperor Viewing Paintings,
*by two European artists working in the Qing court*

accompanied by two cows in a special boat. The Chinese did not use milk in their tea but they knew Macartney liked to do so and they did not want to deprive him.

Back in England, he reported to King George that despite its enormous size, China was a weak country. Poverty was widespread. Although the Emperor and his scholar-officials viewed themselves as highly civilised and culturally superior, they were actually ignorant, fixed in their ways and hopelessly out of date. As Confucians, they looked down on trade and traders, especially barbarian traders. Soldiers still used bows and arrows, swords and spears. Worst of all, nobody seemed interested in progress and everyone was resistant to change.

Lord Macartney was also aware of Han–Manchu tensions. He described the Manchu rulers as 'the tyranny of a handful of Tartars over more than 300 million Chinese'. He noted that the lives of ordinary Chinese were riddled with filth, poverty, disease and supstition. He concluded that China was in decline and was no longer the greatest society in the world.

When Marco Polo visited Kublai Khan in the thirteenth century, he reported that China was the richest and most civilised nation on Earth. When Admiral Zheng He sailed the four seas in his enormous treasure ships 150 years later, China was still way ahead of the West. How did Europe overtake China?

Lord Macartney had seen the three main problems: a poor education system, resistance to change and restriction of trade and new ideas.

There was another reason. In China's highly competitive society, people traditionally kept their inventions secret and seldom published their findings. Some discoveries were passed from father to son but many more were lost or forgotten. Throughout the history of imperial China, there were few books on science and little sharing of knowledge. Unlike Britain, China never established a Royal Society to collect, process and verify scientific findings. Over the centuries, the Chinese lost sight of their own creativity. They invented gunpowder but used it for firework displays instead of war. They were awestruck by Western technology such as guns, clocks and seismographs, having forgotten that China had invented them centuries earlier.

# MISSING: THE THREE Rs AND A ZERO

Education in China was chained to the past and especially weak in scientific thought.

❀ Since the Sui Dynasty, education in China had consisted of learning the *Sayings of Confucius* by heart. Mathematics, science, logic and foreign languages were never taught.

❀ Although paper had been invented in China during the second century and printing in the eighth century, books and maps were not widely available to the general public.

❀ The majority of Chinese people could not read or write because education was privately funded and expensive. There were hardly any publicly funded schools or universities. In Europe, cathedral schools became centres of learning and debate.

❀ Arabic numbers were not adopted in China until the twentieth century. Using Chinese characters to do mathematics was very, very difficult. (Imagine doing multiplication or division with Roman numerals.) As a result, China was backward in mathematics and science. In Europe, Fibonacci's book on Arabic numbers (including the number zero and the importance of placement) showed a simple way to do mathematics.

Western scholars began to discover the laws of physics that governed the universe.

❂ A man's future depended entirely on the results of an imperial examination held every year. Women were not allowed to take the exam. Candidates spent years memorising texts written in 500 BC. Original thinking and debate were not encouraged.

## 2000 YEARS OF EXAMS!

The Imperial Examinations began during the Han Dynasty. A small, elite group of young aristocrats and descendants of prominent officials would be chosen to sit for the exam. The set curriculum consisted of music, arithmetic, writing, knowledge of the rituals, archery and horsemanship. This was later expanded to include military strategy, civil law, revenue and taxation, agriculture, geography, and the Confucian classics.

During the Age of Disunion, the exams were forgotten. They were reinstated by the Sui Emperor. The exams now consisted of written questions which tested the candidates' knowledge of the Confucian classics. For the next 1300 years, the only way to become rich and famous in China was to pass this imperial examination based on the sayings of Confucius. During the Tang Dynasty, aristocrats sent their sons to special schools to get extra coaching. Ordinary people had little chance of sitting for the exam. The First Song Emperor changed this. He wanted everyone to have a chance because of *what* they knew, not *who* they knew. Commoners now had as good an opportunity as the nobles. Everybody studied hard.

The examinations were stopped during the first half of the Yuan Dynasty and then re-started in 1315. However, a quota of only 25 per cent of the degrees would be awarded to the southern Chinese, no matter how well they did. The Chinese thought this was unfair. They eventually rebelled and drove out the Mongols in 1368.

During the Ming Dynasty, 100 000 students took the exams every time they were held. Candidates were locked up in individual cells for several days to write their essays.

Some candidates cheated. Some went on taking the exams aged 60 and over. A few even committed suicide when they failed. The Qing Dynasty schoolteacher Hong Xiuquan never managed to pass the exam. He became so frustrated when he failed for the fourth time that he started a revolution to vent his anger.

The exams were not abolished until 1905.

*Cheat's shirt with 722 essays ready-made for copying*

# MISSING: NEW IDEAS
# AND A NAVY

Under the Southern Song, trade with other countries had flourished. In 1131, money earned from taxing overseas trade made up one-fifth of the Song government's income. During the Yuan Dynasty, shipbuilding and international trade continued to grow. Marco Polo was astonished by the number of boats on the Yangzi River. The Third Ming Emperor had sent a huge fleet under Admiral Zheng He around the world. From the mid-fifteenth century, however, the Ming and Qing banned sea travel and even tried to stop Chinese merchants trading with foreign countries at all.

From then on, China missed out on the stimulus that comes with trade: social contact, new ideas, fresh discoveries in science and technology. She also lost her skills in shipbuilding and navigation. In 1550, a Ming official complained that the knowledge of building large boats had been completely forgotten. Soon the Chinese were unable to defend themselves along the coast, even against Japanese pirates. The late Ming and Qing dynasties became more and more crippled by their own policies.

In the meantime, Dutch, British and French trading companies built their own fleets of gunboats armed with cannons and guns to protect their merchants on the high seas. In time, these ships became powerful enough to make war on any nation which dared to challenge them.

The stage was now set for the Opium War.

# THE OPIUM WAR:
## 'BUY OUR DRUGS, OR ELSE!'

The British were spending so much money buying China's tea, porcelain and silk that all their money was flowing into China. They wanted to sell something to the Chinese in return. That something was opium, a drug extracted from the poppy plant. The British firm East India Trading Company started planting large fields of poppies in India. Although the sale of opium in Britain was frowned on because of its harmful effects, British firms began selling opium to the Chinese. They started with 200 chests of opium in 1729. Sales kept increasing as more and more Chinese became addicted. By 1838, British merchants were selling 40 000 chests of opium to China every year.

The Qing Emperor banned opium smoking in 1813 and made it a crime but the drug was smuggled into China illegally. Finally, the Emperor appointed an honest official, Lin Zexu, as special commissioner to prevent British traders from bringing opium into China. Lin wrote a famous letter to Queen Victoria, saying, 'Let me ask you, where is your conscience? If people from a foreign country were seducing your people into buying and smoking opium, I'm certain you would not be happy either.' He made 20 copies of this letter and asked the captain of every European ship sailing to London to deliver a copy to the Queen of England. She did not reply.

Lin ordered the British superintendent in Canton to collect the chests of opium from British merchants and hand them over. He promptly dumped them into the sea. This so angered the British that they sent a force of 16 warships and 4000 soldiers to teach China a lesson in 1840. China's old-fashioned navy, carrying men armed with spears and swords, was no match for British warships with gleaming cannons. In 1842, China was forced to sign the Treaty of Nanking. Lin was banished to a remote province. Besides paying Britain 21 million ounces of silver, China handed over the island of Hong Kong, fixed the tax on imported goods at 5 per cent, opened five new ports to British traders and granted British citizens living in China the right to be judged by British law and British judges. (This state of affairs lasted until 1949, when the Communist leader Mao Zedong drove out all the foreigners from China. However, Hong Kong was only given back to China in 1997.)

## THE TAIPING REBELLION AND THE PLUNDER OF BEIJING

Chinese people blamed the Manchus for the defeat that led to the Treaty of Nanking. Many decided to rebel. Among them was a village schoolteacher named Hong Xiuquan (pronounced Shiu-chuan). After he failed the imperial examination for the fourth time in 1843, he became furious at the Manchus and decided to drive them out of China.

Hong claimed to be the younger brother of Jesus Christ and started a movement to topple the Manchu government.

Calling himself the heavenly king of a new dynasty (the Taiping, or Heavenly Kingdom of Great Peace), he attracted the peasants from rural China by promising equal division of land and property. In a very short time he had raised a great army. The movement eventually spread over 16 provinces and led to the destruction of 600 cities. Throughout the 1850s, Hong waged war against the Manchus.

In 1856, while the Emperor Xian (pronounced Shian) Feng was battling this massive peasant uprising, the infamous *Arrow* Incident occurred. The *Arrow* was a Chinese-owned junk, manned by a Chinese crew but flying the British flag. In those days, pirate ships around Hong Kong often raided warehouses along the coast of Canton, pretending to be British. Suspecting the *Arrow* of piracy and smuggling, Chinese police boarded the ship, hauled down the flag and arrested twelve Chinese sailors.

Britain protested that the British flag had been insulted and sent 11 000 troops under Lord Elgin. France added 6700 more under General de Montauban. The Emperor and his court fled from Beijing. On 18 October 1860, the Western forces marched into the summer palace called Yuan Ming Yuan (Garden of Perfect Brightness) just outside Beijing.

Built by Emperor Kangxi and his descendants, the Summer Palace consisted of 350 magnificent hectares of hills, ponds, lakes, trails, gardens, pavilions, flowered mazes and palaces.

Famous French writer Victor Hugo described it in a letter:

> There was, in the corner of the world, a wonder . . . a dream with marble, jade, bronze and porcelain . . . frame it with cedar wood, cover it with precious stones, drape it with silk . . . have architects who are poets build the thousand and one dreams of the thousand and one nights . . . suppose a sort of dazzling cavern of human fantasy with the face of a temple and palace, such was this building.

The French arrived first. As one French officer wrote later, it was like the sacking of Rome by the barbarians. The English soon followed. Between them, they left with 300 wagons of loot.

Before departing, Lord Elgin decided to punish the

Emperor in a way he would never forget. He ordered the troops to set fire to the plundered ruins. English officer Charles Gordon wrote to his mother, 'You can scarcely imagine the beauty and magnificence of the places we burnt . . . It was wretchedly demoralizing . . . Everybody was wild for Plunder.'

## UNDER PRESSURE

Fearful of losing his throne, the Emperor ordered his brother, Prince Gong, to negotiate. In desperation Prince

Gong turned to a Russian, Count Nikolai Ignatiev, for advice. The wily Russian agreed to 'help'. He promised Prince Gong that he would make the British and French go away for a price 'to be negotiated later'.

Lord Elgin had himself carried in a red sedan chair through the centre of Beijing into the Audience Hall of the Forbidden Palace. There he and the French insisted that China was to open ten more ports for trade, legalise the opium trade, allow British ships to carry Chinese workers to America and pay a fine of eight million taels of silver.

As soon as they left China, Prince Gong was approached by Count Ignatiev. By then, Prince Gong was exhausted. Without firing a shot or sending a single soldier to China, Ignatiev managed to 'persuade' the prince to hand over 518 000 square kilometres (180 000 square miles) of territory to Russia. It included the entire Amur River basin and 1600 kilometres (1000 miles) of Chinese coast. That very summer, Russia began to build Vladivostok, a port city on the Pacific Ocean.

In Germany, when the terms of the China–Russia Treaty were made public, the writer Friedrich Engels sent a sarcastic note congratulating the Russians for 'dispossessing China of a country as large as France and Germany combined' and doing so without shedding a single drop of blood.

The 30-year-old Emperor Xian Feng died a broken man in August 1861, leaving his six-year-old son to inherit the throne. His concubine Ci Xi travelled to Beijing ahead of all the other ministers, planned a coup and seized power. Ci Xi ruled China for the next 47 years, first through her son, then through her nephew.

And what happened to the Taiping rebels? They held on to Nanjing for 11 years but were defeated when they tried to attack Shanghai. The Taiping leader Hong committed suicide in 1864. The Taiping Rebellion is said to have caused 20 million deaths.

# EMPRESS CI XI
## (PRONOUNCED SUSHI)

Ci Xi was born in 1835, the daughter of a Manchurian official of low rank. When she was 15 years old, she was one of the young Manchu girls chosen to be a consort to the Qing Emperor. Five years later, she gave birth to the Emperor's only son and was promoted to the rank of Noble Consort, second only to the Empress.

In 1860, when Ci Xi was 25, British and French soldiers attacked Beijing. The Emperor fled to his palace in Rehe, Manchuria, with his young son and Ci Xi. On hearing the news that the British and French had looted and burned the Summer Palace, the Emperor became depressed and seriously ill. Knowing he was close to death, he summoned his Empress and his consort Ci Xi and asked them to raise his five-year-old son together. He appointed his best ministers to be the 'Eight Regent Ministers' for his son.

Immediately after his death, Ci Xi persuaded the Empress to become her partner. The two women named themselves co-reigning Empress Dowagers with powers greater than the eight ministers. On their way back to Beijing for the Emperor's funeral, Ci Xi ordered the arrest of the eight for incompetence in dealing with the English and the French. Three were executed and the rest dismissed. Ci Xi's son, Tongzhi, became Emperor. Because he was so young, power remained in the hands of Ci Xi.

The child Emperor grew up to be a playboy. Bored with life in the palace, he began disguising himself as a commoner, sneaking out of the Forbidden Palace at night and visiting prostitutes in brothels. Soon he caught syphilis and became ill. Ci Xi insisted her son had come down with smallpox (both diseases cause a rash). In spite of being treated (for smallpox) by the best doctors, the Emperor died in 1875 at the age of 18.

After her son's death, Ci Xi named her three-year-old nephew to be the next Emperor and adopted him as her son. As a child he was completely dominated by his aunt but later, when he was 27 years old, he ordered a series of reforms which alarmed Ci Xi. Afraid of losing power, she put him under house arrest and proclaimed that he was not fit to be Emperor. She also executed many of his followers.

Two years later, in 1899, the Boxer Rebellion broke out. Angry at China's repeated humiliation at the hands of the Western nations, a group of martial-arts practitioners ('Harmonious Fists' or Boxers) claimed supernatural powers and besieged the Europeans' quarters in Beijing. Against the

Emperor's advice, Ci Xi rashly announced that she supported the rebels. Eight nations joined forces and sent a combined army into Beijing. Alarmed, Ci Xi disguised herself as a peasant and fled to the city of Xian with the puppet Emperor. The allied troops defeated the Boxers and marched into the Forbidden Palace, where they pillaged Ci Xi's private chambers, sprawled on her bed and wrote graffiti on her walls. Her ministers were forced to sign another humiliating peace treaty which included the payment of 67 million British pounds (450 million taels of silver, one tael for each Chinese) to the victors. Only then was Ci Xi allowed to return to Beijing.

Ci Xi did not know this but the eight nations actually had no

intention of toppling her. It suited their purpose very well to have a crippled Qing Dynasty 'in charge' of China.

In November 1908, Ci Xi became ill and knew she was going to die. She ordered the palace eunuchs to give poison to the 37-year-old puppet Emperor (her nephew) who had been kept like a prisoner on an island in the Forbidden Palace for the last ten years. On 14 November 1908, the Emperor died. On the same day, Ci Xi installed her two-year-old grand-nephew as the new Emperor. She herself died the very next day.

In 1911, three years after Ci Xi's death, rebellion broke out throughout China. The six-year-old last Emperor abdicated in 1912 and the Qing Dynasty came to an end. After 3500 years of rule by kings and emperors, China became a republic under Dr Sun Yat-sen.

# DISCOVERY AT DUNHUANG

While the Boxers were attacking foreigners throughout China in 1899, a momentous discovery was being made at a remote cave at the edge of the Gobi Desert.

Wang Yuanlu was a Daoist monk who had spent his life looking after the Caves of a Thousand Buddhas near Dunhuang. One day in 1899, Wang was clearing out a grotto that had been blocked by rocks and sand when he noticed a large crack in the rock. Behind it was a man-made brick wall sealing off an inner chamber. Inside that cavern he saw a huge collection of ancient scrolls, stacked from floor to ceiling.

Wang reported his find to the Governor of Gansu, who was then desperately trying to cope with the Boxer Rebellion in his province. He ordered the monk to re-seal the cave and await further orders.

Seven years later, a mysterious visitor arrived in Dunhuang to call on the monk. Aurel Stein was a Hungarian archaeologist working for the British government in India. He had heard rumours of Wang's amazing library, and had come to see for himself. Stein brought with him a large number of empty crates, and a determination to relieve the monk of some of his treasures.

At their initial meeting in 1906, Stein pretended to be a devout Buddhist from London, bent on a holy pilgrimage in search of sutras (Buddhist texts).

Next day, Stein's Chinese assistant Jiang Xiao-wan persuaded the monk to take down part of the brick wall. Stein later wrote in his book *Ruins of Desert Cathay*: 'There appeared in the dim light of the priest's little lamp a solid mass of manuscript bundles rising to a height of nearly ten feet . . . in a carefully selected rock chamber, hidden behind a brick wall, these masses of manuscripts had lain undisturbed for centuries.' This was true – they had been there for 800 years. The dryness of the climate and darkness within the caves had preserved the murals and manuscripts in their original condition.

Stein was in a fever of excitement, but he was also haunted by the worry that the 'shifty priest . . . would be moved in a sudden fit of alarm or distrust to close down his shell before I had been able to extract any of the pearls'.

The first night, Stein's assistant Jiang carried a few scrolls back to his master carefully hidden in the large sleeves of his Chinese robe 'for closer examination'. Over the next eight nights, three trusted servants delivered sackfuls of manuscripts to Stein's tent to be packed into the empty crates he had so thoughtfully brought along.

Stein was prepared to pay Wang enough money for

Wang 'to retire to his native province and a life of peace'. In the end, his skilful assistant Jiang clinched the deal for a tenth of the amount – only 200 taels. For this paltry sum Stein took away 29 crates filled to the brim. They held 7000 complete manuscripts (including the world's earliest printed book), 6000 fragments, hundreds of embroideries, rare paintings on silk and many other relics.

When Stein took leave of Wang, he departed with the same number of crates he had brought with him. The difference was that now they were full, whereas before they had been empty.

Safely back in England, Stein catalogued his 'purchase' and was staggered. 'When I now survey the wealth of archaeological materials that I carried away, the bargain may well seem great beyond credence.'

A year later, a French scholar arrived and carted away 3000 scrolls to France. Japanese, Russian and American collectors soon followed, each intent on getting his own slice of the pie. The American Langdon Warner (a Harvard professor whose life inspired Hollywood to create Indiana Jones) used glued tapes to peel off 26 of the most beautiful Dunhuang murals and transported them back to America. They are now in the Fogg Art Museum in Boston.

Stein donated his haul to the British Library and the British Museum, and was knighted for his contribution to archaeology.

Sadly, no Chinese dared to protest the wholesale plunder of China's most precious library.

# THE CHINESE LANGUAGE

There are many different dialects of spoken Chinese. The ones most widely used are Mandarin, Cantonese and Hokkien.

- ❀ **MANDARIN** is the dialect of Beijing. It is also the official language of China, supposedly spoken by every Chinese. Besides their local dialect, everyone in China is encouraged to speak Mandarin as a second 'universal' dialect. Why did Mandarin become the official language? Because of history. The Manchus chose Beijing as their capital city when they conquered China in 1644. They learned the local Beijing dialect and called it *Guan Hua* (language of the officials).

- ❀ **CANTONESE** is the dialect of Hong Kong and Guandong Province. Many overseas Chinese in America and Australia emigrated from these two places and speak mainly Cantonese.

- ❀ **HOKKIEN** is the dialect of Fujian Province. It is spoken in Fujian and Taiwan.

All Chinese dialects are tonal languages – the same word spoken in different pitches may mean different things. In Mandarin, there are four tones. Depending on the tone, the word *ma* can mean horse, mother, scold, numb.

*Written* Chinese has no alphabet. Instead each word is a kind of picture (a pictogram), or character.

Long ago, people wrote like this:

| ⺼ | ☉ | 𝅘 | ⊞ |
|------|-----|-----|-------|
| Moon | Sun | Man | Field |

Nowadays the words are written like this:

| 月 | 日 | 人 | 田 |
|------|-----|-----|-------|
| Moon | Sun | Man | Field |

There is no way of knowing how to pronounce a word from the written character. Therefore, a person may know how to read and write Chinese but not how to speak it. British scholar Arthur Waley translated many books from Chinese into English but was unable to speak Chinese.

If there is no alphabet, how can you have a dictionary? In the year 121 AD, during the Han Dynasty, a dictionary called *Shuo Wen* was published. It had 9000 words grouped under 180 basic symbols; such as the symbol for water, wood, bird. This method became the standard for all Chinese dictionaries that came later.

There are about 50 000 Chinese words but you need to know only 3000 of them to be able to read an average book or newspaper. (There are over half a million English words.)

Since there are ten times as many English words as Chinese characters, each Chinese character has to do a lot of work. Each character usually has several meanings. For instance, the word *dao* means road or path. But it also means way, method or doctrine.

What about words that represent ideas? For example, how can a word such as *contradiction* be shown in pictograms?

There is a story about this. A merchant was selling spears and armour in the market place. He boasted that his spears were sharp enough to pierce any armour. Then he claimed that his armour would withstand the thrust of any spear. Someone in the audience asked what would happen if he should use his spear against his own armour. The merchant was unable to answer. Now the two words *mao* (spear) and *dun* (armour) together make (*mao-dun* or spear-armour), which stands for contradiction.

In the same way, two words of opposite meaning (antonyms) are often put together to make a quite different word. For example:

- Business is *mai–mai* or buy–sell
- Size is *da–xiao* or big–small
- How much is *duo–shao* or much–little
- Switch (such as light switch) is *kai–guan* or open-close
- Situation is *chang–duan* or long–short

- Time is *guang–yin* or light–shade
- Object is *dong–xi* or east–west

Other characters use a combination of words to convey an idea. For example, *sheng ren* (raw man) means stranger. What happens when a stranger becomes a friend? He turns into a *shou ren*. Believe it or not, *shou ren* (friend) means COOKED MAN (or ripe man)!

## PROVERBS

The Chinese language is full of proverbs. A proverb is a wise saying that states a general truth or gives a piece of advice. Some proverbs came from Chinese history. For example:

- *Pointing to a deer and calling it a horse* means 'Right and wrong are deliberately mixed up.'

- *Clapping with one hand produces no sound* means 'It takes two people to enter a dialogue.'

- *To plug the ears while stealing the bell* means 'to deceive oneself'.

- *Falling leaves return to their roots* means 'As we age, we go back to our beginnings'.

- *Climbing a tree to seek for fish* means 'attempting to do the impossible'.

# SOME WORDS TO AVOID IN MANDARIN

Translated into English, these phrases don't sound bad, but don't say them to a Chinese in Mandarin!

- ❀ Most common is *ta ma de*. It means his mother's. Equivalent to damn, or worse.
- ❀ *Wang ba* means *turtle*. A turtle does not know its father – a bad insult.
- ❀ *Wang ba dan* means egg of turtle – also quite rude.
- ❀ *Dan* means egg and is often part of an insult.
  *bun dan* means stupid egg or dummy
  *hun dan* means mixed-up egg or idiot
  *dao dan* means to topple an egg or cause trouble
  *huai dan* means bad egg or an evil person
  *gun dan* means rolling egg or get lost
  *hutu dan* means confused egg or fool
  *qiong guang dan* means poor naked egg or penniless beggar
- ❀ *Gua* means melon and is also used as an insult.
  *Sha gua* means dumb melon or blockhead or simpleton.
- ❀ *Za zong* means cross-breed. A racist slur.
- ❀ *Fei hua* means useless phrase. Equivalent to rubbish.

- *Bu yao lian* means not want face. Equivalent to shameless.
- *Hu li jing* means fox spirit. Equivalent to sly woman.
- *Gong gong qi che* means public bus. Equivalent to woman without morals.
- *Fang pi* means to go fart. Originated during Yuan Dynasty. Equivalent to nonsense or rubbish.
- *Dai lu mao* means wearing green hat. Equivalent to cuckold. In the Tang Dynasty, brothels employed male attendants to introduce men to prostitutes. These hired hands wore green hats to tell them apart from valued customers. It's best not to give green hats to Chinese men.

# NO MORE EMPERORS?

1912 TO TODAY
CAPITAL CITY: BEIJING

**After World War II, the Communist Party ruled China. The most powerful man was Mao Zedong, who unified the country but caused millions of deaths and great suffering. After Mao, China opened its doors, and transformed itself into a modern nation.**

The history of China during the twentieth century was dominated by the lives of four men: a doctor, a professional soldier and two Communist revolutionaries.

## KIDNAPPED IN LONDON

The doctor, Dr Sun Yat-sen (1866–1925), was born to a peasant family in a coastal village near Macau in southern China. When he was 13 years old, he left China to live with his brother who had emigrated to Honolulu and become a successful merchant. He learned English, converted to Christianity and was one of the first two medical graduates of the newly established Hong Kong College of Medicine, where he was taught by the Scottish professor James Cantlie. Instead of practicing medicine, Sun decided to devote himself to overthrowing the Qing Dynasty. After a failed uprising in 1895, he became a fugitive in China. He cut off his queue (pigtail), grew a moustache and put on a Western suit before fleeing abroad and spent the next 16 years organising a secret society to turn China into a republic.

Unaware that the Manchu authorities were watching his every move, Dr Sun was lured into the Chinese Embassy in London on the morning of 11 October 1896 and placed under house arrest. Terrified of being shipped back to China where he expected to be chopped into a thousand pieces, Sun appealed in desperation to the two English servants guarding him. After a week of anxious days and sleepless nights, the two domestics finally agreed to deliver a letter to Sun's teacher James Cantlie, who was in London at the time. Cantlie promptly contacted a reporter at London's newspaper, the *Globe*.

'Surprising News!' the *Globe* reported in a special edition. 'Revolutionist kidnapped and detained in London's Chinese Embassy!' The bulletin shocked the nation. Journalists rushed to the Embassy. They interviewed Cantlie at home. Scotland Yard sent detectives to investigate. The British Prime Minister, Lord Salisbury, protested that China had violated international law. Fearful of causing an incident, the Chinese Ambassador relented and released Dr Sun unharmed.

When Dr Sun walked out of the Embassy onto the London streets, he found himself famous. His name had become a household word. Still he did not dare to return to China. Instead, he stayed in London and wrote a book titled *Kidnapped in London*. The book was translated into many languages and further enhanced his reputation throughout the world.

In 1911, a bomb exploded by accident in the quarters of army officers planning an uprising in the city of Wuhan. Afraid of being exposed, the officers seized the arsenal at gunpoint and declared their independence. Within six weeks, 16 provinces had joined the revolt. A year later, the six-year-old Qing Emperor gave up his throne and China became a republic.

Dr Sun was in Denver, Colorado when the imperial government collapsed. He hurried back and was elected president of the Chinese Nationalist Party or Kuomingtang (KMT). It was a chaotic time with numerous warlords fighting one another for control. In order to avoid bloodshed, Dr Sun gave up his leadership to Yuan Shikai, Commander-in-Chief of the Qing army. Yuan persuaded the last Qing Emperor to abdicate before assuming presidency of the Republic of China. He tried to make himself Emperor but died of kidney failure in 1916.

In 1917, Russia became Communist after a revolution. The Communists promised that Russia would become a classless society in which everyone was equal and there would be no private ownership of property. Communism spread to China and a Chinese Communist Party was founded in 1921. Mao Zedong was one of its first members.

Dr Sun decided that his KMT party needed to include members of the Chinese Communist Party (CCP) as allies. His protégé and successor, the professional soldier Chiang Kai-shek, disagreed. Dr Sun died of liver cancer in 1925 and General Chiang took over leadership of the KMT. Legend has it that Chiang proposed to Dr Sun's widow but she refused to marry him. Undaunted, Chiang married the widow's younger sister instead.

# THE GENERAL AND THE LIBRARIAN

General Chiang Kai-shek (1887–1975) was a career army officer from Zhejiang Province. His merchant father had died when he was only three years old. He studied military science in Japan and served in the Japanese Imperial Army until 1911, when he went back to China and helped found the KMT with Dr Sun. After Sun's death, Chiang became head of the KMT. In April 1927, General Chiang seized control by suddenly launching a 'party purification' program in Shanghai. He persuaded members of the powerful local Green Gang to hunt down and kill all the Communist labour organisers. Many were awakened from a sound sleep in the dark of night and gunned down in their beds. Their leader, Comrade Mao Zedong, escaped to the countryside while General Chiang's KMT established their power base in the cities. Chiang and Mao became mortal enemies.

Seven years later, in 1934, the Communists were on the verge of being hunted down and destroyed by the KMT.

Under the leadership of Mao Zedong, they retreated on foot to China's west, then north. After walking for 370 days over 13 000 kilometres (8000 miles) of difficult terrain, they finally settled in the remote caves of Yanan in Shaanxi Province. Only 10 per cent of the marchers survived. This epic journey is called the Long March.

Mao Zedong (1893–1976) was the eldest son of a peasant from Hunan Province. His father had had only two years of schooling and his mother was illiterate, but Mao was a good student and loved to read. He graduated from high school and followed his teacher to Beijing. There he worked as an assistant librarian at Beijing University and sat in on many classes. He married his teacher's daughter and joined the Communist Party in 1921. In 1930, his wife and young son were captured by the Nationalists (the KMT) and his wife was executed. Mao rose to become the leader and chairman of the Chinese Communist Party.

Throughout his life, he fancied himself as a poet as well as a revolutionary. A collection of his sayings was published in *The Little Red Book*, which was read like a bible during the Cultural Revolution of the 1960s. Mao believed that support for the Communist Party would come from the peasants in the countryside, not the industrial workers in the city.

# WHICH WAY CHINA?
# TWO DIFFERENT PATHS

As a career soldier, General Chiang wanted to build a strong army, defeat the warlords, unite China, end the unequal treaties with the West, and win the war against Japan. Coming from a landlord-merchant family, he wanted to work with the West, develop trade and industries and establish KMT rule throughout China.

What did Mao want? The opposite! As the ruthless son of a clever peasant, he wanted to get rid of the landlords and merchants (and throw out General Chiang and his KMT), expel the foreigners for good, empower peasants, confiscate all the land for the state and reduce the influence of the West. He wanted China to be a classless, Communist society with himself as Chairman and Supreme Ruler until death.

The thing they both wanted was a strong, independent China free from Western colonialism. During World War II, the United States persuaded General Chiang and Comrade Mao to join forces and fight against Japan. After World War II ended, Chiang and Mao fought each other in a bitter civil war for four years. Chiang was defeated and fled to Taiwan in 1949. After that, Mao Zedong ruled China for 27 years. He kicked out all the foreigners and closed China's doors to the outside world.

# KOXINGA AND FORMOSA (TAIWAN)

The history of Taiwan is intimately linked with the life of the legendary 'founder' of Taiwan: the seventeenth-century Chinese pirate Koxinga.

Koxinga was a Ming Dynasty loyalist born in Japan in 1624 to a Chinese father and Japanese mother. His real name was Zheng Cheng Gong. After the last Ming Emperor committed suicide in 1644, Koxinga rallied around Prince Tang, one of the Ming princes, to fight the Manchu invaders. Prince Tang treated Koxinga like a son and allowed him to use the royal surname. (The name Koxinga came from the Dutch pronunciation of Zheng's Chinese nickname Guo Xing Ye which means 'lord of the imperial surname'.)

After the defeat and capture of Prince Tang in 1661, Koxinga escaped to the island of Formosa (now called Taiwan) with 400 ships and 25 000 troops. In those days it was a rural place with few inhabitants, mostly indigenous people. Dutch traders had made it a Dutch colony 37 years earlier. Koxinga decided to drive out the Dutch and use the island as a base to continue his fight against the Manchus. After a nine-month siege, Koxinga became the ruler of Formosa. Unfortunately, he caught malaria and died four months later.

Formosa was ruled by Koxinga's son and grandson for the next 20 years during which over 100 000 Chinese emigrated there, mostly from neighbouring Fujian Province. A Qing general eventually conquered Formosa in 1683 and Ming resistance to Qing rule ended for good.

Two hundred years later in 1895, Japan handed China a crushing defeat in a war over Korea. As a result, Formosa became a Japanese colony. Hungry for more land and power, Japan invaded mainland China in the 1930s. During World War II, the United States persuaded Mao and Chiang to join forces to fight Japan, their common enemy.

After Japan's defeat in 1945, Taiwan was returned to China. In 1949, Chiang fled there with two million followers and remained there until his death in 1975. His son, Chiang Ching-guo, then became president and ruled Taiwan until 1988. Towards the end of his rule, the younger Chiang allowed democratic elections to be held. At present there are two political parties, the Nationalist Party (mostly those who followed Chiang to Taiwan after 1949) and the Democratic Progressive Party (mostly those who had settled there before 1949, descendants of Koxinga's followers).

Since 1988, democratic elections have been held every four years. Taiwan has a population of 23 million.

# GREAT LEAP BACKWARDS?

For 27 years between 1949 and his death in 1976, Chairman Mao was the pre-eminent leader and most powerful man in China. Seldom in the history of mankind has one man so dominated a country.

Chairman Mao began by getting rid of all the landlords. Reputedly, 700 000 died. He proclaimed that all land now belonged to the 'people'. In reality, everyone worked for the state. Communes were established throughout China. (A commune consisted of a large group of people, not all of the same family, living together and sharing income, property and responsibilities.) These communes had annual grain quotas which had to be filled and handed over to the state before anyone could get his own ration of grain.

In 1958, Mao began the movement known as the Great Leap Forward. Its purpose was to transform China into an industrial country overnight. Hundreds of thousands of furnaces were built in the back yards of peasants' homes to produce steel. Unfortunately, most of the steel produced this way was not usable.

The next year, 1959, there was a poor harvest. Party members reported false, inflated figures for grain production in order to please Mao. Government collection of grain increased despite reduced grain yields. Thirty million peasants died from famine, malnutrition and disease.

Marshal Peng, a war hero, actually dared to criticise Mao at a conference in 1959. A vengeful Chairman Mao demoted Peng and placed him under house arrest. Later, Peng was tortured and killed.

As he grew older, Mao behaved more and more like an emperor. His third wife, a former actress, blindly carried out his wishes and tolerated his affairs. He lived in the old imperial palace in Beijing known as Zhongnanhai (Central and South Lakes). According to his doctor, Li Zhisui, Mao never brushed his teeth but merely rinsed his mouth with green tea. By the age of 70, most of his teeth had fallen out. The few that remained were covered in green slime. He disliked bathing but allowed himself to be wiped with hot, moist towels. He enjoyed dancing and had many young mistresses. Although he suffered from a mild form of venereal disease, he never had it treated. Towards the end of his life, he spent a lot of time in bed, not bothering to get dressed for days at a time.

*Monument outside the Mao Zedong Memorial Hall, Tiananmen Square, Beijing*

# ATTACKING THE FOUR OLDS

In June 1966, Chairman Mao launched the 'Cultural Revolution' to demote his fellow party members who were in power and to show off his supremacy. He closed all the middle schools and universities throughout the country. Teenagers were encouraged to wear red armbands, wave little red books filled with the sayings of Mao and attack the four 'olds': old customs, old habits, old ideas and old culture. They called themselves Red Guards and terrorised the land.

# CONFESSIONS WHILE KNEELING ON GLASS

The Red Guards travelled on trains and buses for free, abused and beat their teachers, defied their parents, burned foreign books, destroyed antiques and public monuments and invaded stores and homes. Professors, scholars, writers, ministers and all authority figures were publicly insulted and forced to make confessions of wrong-doing while kneeling on broken glass in front of their student-torturers. Many were killed. Still more committed suicide. The only person immune from attack was Chairman Mao. Everyone else was purged, including the former Chief of State, the Premier and the Secretary-General of the Party.

For approximately ten years until Mao's death in

September 1976, there was poverty and chaos throughout China. This period of history, including the worst years of the Cultural Revolution between 1966 and 1969 when hundreds of thousands died, is still painful and is seldom discussed in public or taught in schools in China.

Despite the widespread misery during the last ten years of his life, Mao is still revered by many people in China. After Mao's death his successor, Deng Xiaoping, judged him to have been 70 per cent right and 30 per cent wrong. Mao united the country and freed it from foreign domination. He built a strong army and gave women equal rights. He had the personality and the will to centralise control, creating a united administration for his successor, Deng, to launch his reforms. Without Mao, China might have become a fragmented country ruled by warlords. The present government recognises Mao's contribution and his photo adorns all the banknotes issued by the Bank of China today.

## QUIET ACHIEVER

Of the four men whose lives re-shaped China during the twentieth century, the fourth man, Deng Xiaoping (1904–1997), was the least known but accomplished the most. Many Asians consider Deng to have been the most influential man of the twentieth century.

Deng Xiaoping (pronounced Shiao-ping) was born to an educated middle-class family in Sichuan Province. His father had studied law and political science. At the age of 16, Deng went to France on a work-study program and stayed there for five years. In 1924, he joined the Chinese Communist Party. Before returning to China, Deng spent a year in a Moscow university where one of his classmates was the son of General Chiang Kai-shek. The younger Chiang eventually became president of Taiwan.

Deng returned to China in 1926 and gradually rose to become General Secretary of the Central Committee in the 1950s. During the Cultural Revolution in 1966, Mao dismissed Deng from all his posts, labelled him a capitalist sympathiser and sent him to do manual labour in a remote area. Deng's son, a physics student at Beijing University, was pushed out of a building and became permanently paralysed from the waist down.

After the death of Mao in 1976, there was a power struggle between Deng and Mao's widow, leader of the legendary Gang of Four who had assumed power and oppressed China during the Cultural Revolution. Deng emerged triumphant as China's top leader. Mao's widow later committed suicide while in prison.

Almost immediately, Deng launched his program of reforms that triggered China's amazing transformation. He began by giving land back to the peasants. Farmers were free to grow anything they wished on their family plots provided they delivered a specified quota of crops to the government. 'To grow rich is glorious!' Deng proclaimed. Within a few years, the communes were dismantled. Hundreds of millions of peasants returned to family farming and escaped poverty through personal drive and hard work. Life became suddenly full of hope.

Calling his reforms 'socialism with Chinese characteristics', Deng deliberately withdrew the Communist Party's authority on many aspects of daily life while opening China's doors to the outside world. Besides encouraging trade with foreign countries, Deng established special economic zones and joint ventures with foreigners along China's coast, especially in the areas close to Hong Kong and Macau. By the late 1990s, the south-east coast of China had become one of the most dynamic and fastest-growing regions in the world.

In 1984, Deng held talks with British Prime Minister Margaret Thatcher about the return of Hong Kong to China in 1997. Deng agreed that after the handover, Hong Kong should be governed according to British law for a period of 50 years. It was Deng who coined the famous phrase 'One Country Two Systems'.

On the political front, Deng introduced regulations to limit the terms of political office. Nobody was allowed tenure for life. The General Secretary (president) and the Prime Minister were to serve a maximum of two five-year terms. Deng chose his own successor (Jiang Zemin) who served from 1993 to 2003. He also suggested Hu Jintao, a graduate in engineering from China's best university, as

Jiang's successor. Students at Beijing University joke among themselves that China is presently being ruled by the Communist Dynasty according to the will of Uncle Deng.

Jiang continued Deng's economic reforms until his retirement in 2003, when he confirmed Deng's candidate, Hu Jintao, as president. Hu has continued to maintain tight political control while liberalising the economy. There is still only one party in China, the Communist Party.

In October 2007, it was announced that Xi Jinping will probably be the next President (China's fifth) after 2112. Xi (pronounced She) has a degree in chemical engineering and is the son of a high-ranking party member. The nomination of Xi represents China's continued peaceful transition of leadership from elderly survivors of the Long March to young, well-educated and pragmatic technocrats.

# SLEEPING DRAGON WAKES

China has changed more since the death of Mao in 1976 than in the 2000 years that preceded it. More people can read now than ever before. Women have the same rights as men, as well as equal opportunity in their careers. Life expectancy has soared. Energy and optimism are evident everywhere. Over 200 million peasants have moved from the countryside to work in the cities. The booming economy of China is based more and more on industry rather than agriculture. China is fast emerging as manufacturer to the entire world. There is no doubt in anyone's mind that this land of dragons and emperors will be a superpower in the twenty-first century. But exactly what kind of society it will be is harder to predict.

In 2008 the Olympics took place in Beijing for the first time in history. It was magnificent and hugely successful. The centre of gravity of the world's economy is tilting increasingly towards India and China. As the world changes, 'hybrids' like myself who were born in China but live in the West can only hope that the new generation of Chinese leaders will seize their moment and make their mark in history with honour and justice.

Philosopher George Santayana wrote, 'Those who cannot remember the past are condemned to repeat it.' I would add that for East and West to get along, they must know and understand one another's history. I hope this book will make a small contribution towards that understanding.

# TIMELINE

**1.6 million to 20 000 years ago**   Paleolithic period, or Old Stone Age
Peking Man (*Homo erectus* or 'man who stood straight') used stone tools
and fire and lived as hunter-gatherers.

**20 000 to 5000 years ago**   Neolithic period, or New Stone Age
Neolithic man planted grain for food, formed villages, domesticated
animals and made pottery.

### 3000–2070 BC   Mythical 'Time of Three Sovereigns and Five Emperors'
Invention of silk weaving. Primitive form of writing carved on rocks.
Chinese mythology says a few brilliant men taught and civilised the people
during this period. *Fu Xi* domesticated animals and cooked with fire.
*Shen Nong*, the divine farmer, invented the plough for farming. He boiled
water before drinking, invented tea-drinking and used herbs as medicines.
*Yellow Emperor* built boats, invented the wheel and wrote a book on
internal medicine. His wife was the goddess of silk. *Cang Jie* saw birds
leaving their claw prints on sand and invented Chinese characters.

### 2070–1600 BC   Xia Dynasty
Stone tools still used, along with pottery and bronze vessels.

### 1600–1122 BC   Shang Dynasty | *House of Yin*
Settled farming (growing millet, wheat, rice and hemp) widespread.
Chinese writing on oracle bones. Cowrie shells used as money.

### 1122–256 BC   Western & Eastern Zhou Dynasties | *House of Ji*
The Jis claimed that natural disasters and rebellions against the Yins
proved that the Yins had lost their Mandate of Heaven (divine right to rule)
to the Jis.

WESTERN ZHOU (1127–771 BC), *capital city Xian*
First copper coinage. Writing with brush and ink on wood, bamboo or silk. The Jis sent their relatives and generals to conquer nearby territories and govern them as lords. Much fighting among these lords. In 771 BC, some of the lords rebelled against the Zhou.

EASTERN ZHOU (771–256 BC), *capital city Luoyang*
The Ji royal family fled east and established a new capital in Luoyang. This period was divided into:

Spring and Autumn Period (771–481 BC)
The Zhou dynasty granted numerous lords the right to rule separate little kingdoms. These lords fought one another. The stronger conquered the weaker and became bigger. Confucius (551–479 BC) lived at this time.

Warring States Period (481–221 BC)
The different states kept fighting one another with the stronger ones conquering the weaker ones and becoming bigger. State of Qin eliminated the Zhou Dynasty in 256 BC. By then, only seven states were left. In the next 35 years, Qin conquered the other six states and united China in 221 BC.

**221–206 BC   Qin Dynasty** | *House of Ying, capital near Xian*
The King of Qin took the title First Emperor of China. First Emperor standardised coins, measurements, and writing throughout the country. He built 6500 kilometres (4000 miles) of roads, the Great Wall, canals, bridges and palaces and the biggest tomb in the world.

**206 BC – 220 AD   Han Dynasty** | *House of Li, capital city Xian*
Trade began along the Silk Road. Grand Historian, Sima Qian (145–90 BC) wrote *Historical Record*. Cast and wrought iron, metal stirrups, the magnetic compass, bronze seismograph and paper invented. First paper handkerchief (nose-wiper or Kleenex).

**220–589 AD   Age of Disunion**
Many short-lived dynasties and kingdoms fighting one another. Nomads

from Mongolia and Manchuria invaded China and settled there. The people turned to religion and became Buddhists or Daoists. First cave murals painted at Dunhuang – Buddhist paintings and sculptures. Invention of matches.

## 589–618 AD   Sui Dynasty | *House of Yang, capital city Xian*
Reunited China. Buddhist faith encouraged. Palaces, highways and extension of Great Wall completed. Building of the Grand Canal caused loss of many lives. Four failed campaigns against Korea, and one against Vietnam.

## 618–907 AD   Tang Dynasty | *House of Li, capital city Xian*
China's only woman 'Emperor' gave women many new freedoms. Population over 50 million. The world's first printed book – golden age for writing and the arts. Sports included a kind of football, archery, polo, cockfighting, cricket-fighting.

## 907–960 AD   Five Dynasties and Ten Kingdoms
Many short-lived dynasties and kingdoms arose during this period as rival warlords and army commanders fought for power. North China was ruled by a succession of five brief dynasties while South China was divided into ten kingdoms.

## 960–1279 AD   Song Dynasty
This period was divided into:
NORTHERN SONG (960–1127 AD), *capital city Kaifeng*
SOUTHERN SONG (1127–1279 AD), *capital city Hangzhou*
Ruled by a scholar elite, the Song despised their own army. The Jin from Manchuria defeated them, kidnapped the last two Song emperors and occupied North China. A different branch of the dynasty then took over in the south. Rice became a staple for southern Chinese. Woodblock printing used to print books and paper money. Many new inventions including clocks, windmills, gunpowder, rockets, bombs, canal locks, movable type and a postal system. Footbinding for women introduced.

**1279–1368 AD   Yuan Dynasty** | *The Khans from Mongolia, capital city Beijing*

Horses, gunpowder and trebuchets used by the Mongols to defeat the Chinese and many other countries. Kublai's palace in Beijing built. Marco Polo's book about his travels published. Tea widely drunk. Cotton introduced.

**1368– 1644 AD   Ming Dynasty** | *House of Zhu, capital city Beijing*

Eunuchs powerful in government. Voyages of Admiral Zheng He and his treasure fleet, followed by ban on foreigners' visits and trade. Blue-and-white porcelain made from cobalt imported from Persia. Great Wall extended and rebuilt.

**1644–1912 AD   Qing Dynasty** | *House of Aisin Gioro from Manchuria, capital city Beijing*

Chinese forced to wear pigtails by Manchu rulers. Opium war with the British exposed Qing military weakness. Taiping Revolution. Plunder of Beijing by British and French soldiers. Boxer Rebellion. Discovery of caves at Dunhuang. Last Emperor abdicates.

**1912–1949 AD   Republic of China**

China under Nationalist Party ruled by Sun Yat-sen and Chiang Kai-shek till 1949. Communist Mao Zedong defeated Chiang Kai-shek and drove him to Taiwan.

**1949 – today   Communist China**

Chairman Mao's Great Leap Forward a failure. Cultural Revolution led to widespread violence and killing. Mao's successor Deng Xiaoping established economic reforms after Mao's death. China gradually became an industrial and financial powerhouse. Population 1.3 billion.

# WHERE TO FIND OUT MORE

Arthur Cotterell and Laura Buller, *Ancient China*, Dorling Kindersley, 2005
Arthur Cotterell, *China*, Dorling Kindersley, 2006. (A new edition by Hugh
    Sebag-Montefiore will be available soon)
Stephen Keeler, *The Changing Face of China*, Hachette, 2007
John S. Major, *The Silk Route: 7,000 Miles of History*, HarperCollins, 1996
Jane O'Connor, *The Emperor's Silent Army*, Viking, 2002
Julia Waterlow, *The Real World: China*, Hachette, 2006
Suzanne Williams, *Made in China: Ideas and Inventions from Ancient
    China*, Pacific View Press, 1996

http://idp.bl.uk/
http://chinaknowledge.de/
http://china-inc.com/education/
http://www.thechinaguide.com/

## For adults
May-Lee & Winberg Chai, *China A to Z*, Plume Books, 2007
*China: People Place Culture History*, Dorling Kindersley, 2007
Patricia Buckley Ebrey, *The Cambridge Illustrated History of China*,
    University of Cambridge Press, 1996
Jonathan Fenby, ed., *The Seventy Wonders of China*, Thames & Hudson,
    2007
Bamber Gascoigne, *The Dynasties of China*, Constable & Robinson, 2003
Harry G. Gelber, *The Dragon and the Foreign Devil*, Allen & Unwin, 2005
Grant Hardy & Anne Behnke Kinney, *The Establishment of the Han Empire
    and Imperial China*, Greenwood Press, 2005
*Inside China*, National Geographic Society, 2007
John Man, *The Terracotta Army*, Transworld, 2007
Robert Murowchick (ed.), *China: Ancient Culture, Modern Land*,
    University of Oklahoma Press, 1994
Joseph Needham, *Science and Civilisation in China*, Cambridge University
    Press, ongoing series
Jonathan Spence, *Memory Palace of Matteo Ricci*, Penguin, 1985
Robert Temple, *The Genius of China*, Touchstone, 1986
Arthur Waley, *The Opium War through Chinese Eyes*, Stanford University
    Press, 1958
Frances Wood, *The Silk Road: Two Thousand Years in the Heart of Asia*,
    University Presses of California, Columbia and Princeton, 2003
Michael Yamashita and William Lindesay, *The Great Wall: From Beginning
    to End*, Sterling, 2007
Adeline Yen Mah, *A Thousand Pieces of Gold*, HarperCollins, 2002

# ACKNOWLEDGEMENTS

The publisher would like to thank the following for images used in the text:

Tony Link Design dragon image vi–viii and chapter openers; Masterfile iii lantern; Blackred Images p4, 7–11 Chinese calligraphy; Getty Images p19 statues (Keren Su); p36 man on horseback (Bridgeman Art Library); Andrew Plant maps pp14–5, pp122–3; p191 detail of cribbing robe used in imperial examinations, courtesy of the East Asian Library and the Gest Collection, Princeton University, photograph by Heather Larkin

iStockphoto.com and named photographers
p5 stone dragon on wall in Forbidden City, Beijing (Kenliang Wong); p6 Chinese zodiac (Leong Kin Fei); p8 number on door (Natalia Bratslavsky), lucky knot with vintage coins (emily2k); p21 terracotta warriors (Ke Wang); p23 terracotta warriors (Thomas Kuest); p24 terracotta warriors (Valerie Crafter); p43 statue of Confucius (Gautier Willaume); p61 calligrapher's hands (Elena Ray); p98 Spring Festival lanterns (Zhu Difeng); p135 Mongol warrior (ELabStudio); pp160-1 Forbidden City, Beijing (Bernard Loic); p179 Great Wall watchtower (Photo2easy, Inc); p185 ancient coins (J. Tan), p223 monument outside Mao Zedong Memorial Hall, Tiananmen Square, Beijing (Alan Crawford)

wikimedia commons/public domain
v Tang Court (Louis le Grand); x–xi Temple of Heaven, Beijing (Maros Mraz); p2 wall roof modelled as dragon, Yu Yuan Gardens, Shanghai (Miguel A. Monjas); p3; Chinese dragon, engraving on wood (Bibliothèque des Arts décoratifs, Paris; Rama); flag of the Qing Dynasty, 1889 (Hoshie); p4 two dragons, Qingyanggong temple, Chengdu (Felix Andrews); p11 yellow dragon robe of Emperor Qianlong, (Grassi Museum, Leipzig, Germany; Dr Meierhofer); p13 court ladies preparing silk (Jonathan Gross); p18 Qin Shihuang (Miuki); p20 Qin Shihuang (Paul Halsell, Brooklyn College website); p34 Liu Bang (Miuki); p35 terracotta figure (Musée Guimet, Paris; Vassil); p38 jade pendant (Musée Guimet, Paris; Vassil); p39 lamp (Shizhao); p44 Confucius on his way to Luoyang (Louis le Grand); p45 Sima Qian (Shizhao); p46 bamboo book, Sun Tzu, *The Art of War* (Special Collection, University of California Riverside; vlasta2/Coelacan); p47 Han earthenware figure (Musée Guimet, Paris; Vassil); p48 horse head (Musée Guimet, Paris; Vassil); p52 Zhang Heng (Periclesof Athens), seismograph (Shizhao); p53 odometer (tomb relief, Imperial Palace, Beijing); p56 rock-cut Buddha sculpture, Longmen Caves, Luoyang (Aberlin); p57 jar (PHG ; Shanghai Museum); p59 Buddhist statues, Dragon Gate Cave, Luoyang (Fanghong); p66 Westerner on camel (Shanghai Museum; PHGCOM); p71 horse and rider, Tang painting (www.chinapage.org); p73 Tang court ladies (Louis le Grand); p77 Emperor Taizong (Louis le Grand);

p79 Emperor Gaozong (Kavino7); p81 Giant Wild Goose Pagoda, Xian (Alex Kwok); p83 Emperor Tang Xuanzong (Louis le Grand); p84–5 Tang terracotta dancers, polo player, figurine (Musée Guimet, Paris; Vassil); p86 polo players (Louis le Grand); p87 Yang Guifei (Seikado Bunko Art Museum, Tokyo; Kaznov17); p90 section of Ming scroll painting (Freer Gallery of Art, Smithsonian Institution, Washington D.C., Purchase – B.Y. Lam Foundation Fund F1993.4, detail; PericlesofAthens); p100 distinguished scholar (Yorck Project); p103 Emperor Huizong (Hardouin/ Fanghong), Huizong's painting (Immanuel Giel); p104 Emperor Huizong and his painting 'Listening to the Qin' (Zhao Ji); p105 'The Broken Balustrade', Gaozong's court (Yorck Project); p110 Yue Fei (Hannah); p114 statue of Yue Fei (Dice/Shizhao); p117 sandstone pillow (Musée Guimet, Paris; Vassil); p118 Song Dynasty junk (PHGCOM); Song river ship (Wandalstouring, courtesy of *Chinese Siege Warfare: Mechanical Artillery & Siege Weapons of Antiquity* by Liang Jieming); p126 statue of Genghis Khan, Dadal Sum (Chineeb); p128 portrait of Kublai Khan, National Palace Museum, Taiwan (Shizhao); p129 Kublai Khan on hunting expedition, silk handscroll, Liu Guandao, 1280 (Latebird); p131 Beijing's drum tower viewed from bell tower (David Balch); p132 three-quarter view of trebuchet (.:Ajvol:.); side view of trebuchet (.:Ajvol:.); p133 replica of trebuchet (Château de Catelnaud, France; Lviatour); p137 Polos in Bukhara (PHGCOM); p139 Polos returning to Kubilai with gifts from Pope Gregory X (PHGCOM); p140 page from *Travels of Marco Polo* (Chris 73); Columbus's notes on Polo's *Le Livre des Merveilles* (PHGCOM); p141 manuscript copy of Yuan imperial edict (Latebird); p142 Moon Festival flag (Allen Timothy Chang); p145 formula for gunpowder (PericlesofAthens); p146 fire-ships, fire-lance, rocket, naval mine (PericlesofAthens); p150 Zhu Yuanzhang (Hardouin/ Shizhao); p152 Zhu Di (Louis le Grand); p154 Zhu Di observing eunuchs playing cuju (Louis le Grand); p159 map of Zheng He's voyages (Liftarn, PHGCOM); p166 Ming dragon plate (Musée Guimet, Paris; Vassil), Ming earthernware jar (Musée Guimet, Paris; Vassil); p168 Matteo Ricci (Shizhao); p169 Matteo Ricci's gravestone in Beijing (Snowyowls); p170 Emperor Wanli (Thomas Pusch); p174 court ladies, silk scroll, Tang Yin (Palace Museum, Beijing; Kaznov17); p175 Great Wall, Mutianyu (Ahazan/D-Kuru); p176 Great Wall, Mutianyu (Ahazan/D-Kuru); p182 Emperor Shunzhi (Highshines); p183 Emperor Kangxi, hanging silk scroll (Palace Museum, Beijing; Gryffindor); p184 Kangxi on tour (Louis le Grand); p186 young Emperor Qianlong, by Guiseppe Castiglione (Louis le Grand), *Qianlong Emperor Viewing Paintings*, by Guiseppe Castiglione and Ding Guanpeng (Palace Museum, Beijing; Gryffindor); p187 Ming plates (Musée Guimet, Paris; Vassil); p195 Hong Xiuquan (contemporary drawing, c. 1860; Dr Meierhofer); p196 Summer Palace, Beijing (composite panorama, Adam Luter 2002); p197 Summer Palace (Shizhao); p198 Prince Gong (Felice Beato, 1860; Chat-rat); p199 Prince Gong (Highshines); p201 Empress Dowager Ci Xi, c.1890 (Highshines); p202 Empress Dowager Ci Xi, c.1890 (Louis le Grand); p214 Sun Yat-sen at 17 (itsmine); p217 Chiang Kai-shek, 1945 (Gelo71), Mao Zedong, 1939 (Spencer195); p218 Mao Zedong (Vancouverguy); p221 Koxinga statue, Anping (Rintojiang/Shunzhao); p225 Deng Xiaoping, 1979 (Borisblue)

# INDEX

# Adeline Yen Mah

was born in Tianjin, China, and trained to be a doctor in London. She had a distinguished career in medicine in the United States for many years. In 1997 she published her memoir, *Falling Leaves*, which was a worldwide bestseller and was translated into eighteen languages. *Chinese Cinderella* is her memoir for young adults. She is also the author of *Chinese Cinderella and the Secret Dragon Society*. She is delighted to hear from readers at her Web site, www.adelineyenmah.com.

Adeline is married to the artist Robert A. Mah. They have two grown children and divide their time between Los Angeles, London, Shanghai, and Hong Kong.